MY THOUSAND AND ONE DAYS

FARAH, SHAHBANOU OF IRAN

My Thousand and One Days

an Autobiography

TRANSLATED FROM THE FRENCH BY
FELICE HARCOURT

55651

W. H. ALLEN · LONDON
A Howard & Wyndham Company
1978

Film set in 11/12 point Palatino
Printed and bound in Great Britain
by W & J Mackay Limited, Chatham
for the Publishers, W. H. Allen & Co. Ltd.,
44 Hill Street, London W1X 8LB

ISBN 0 491 02146 1

Contents

Illustrations

7

With President and Mrs Carter (Photo: Diana Walker, Camera Press London)
The First Queen to be Crowned (Photo: Popperfoto)
After the Coronation (Photo: Keystone Press)
An Official Coronation Photograph (Photo: Rex Features)
Receiving the Chinese Vice-Premier (Photo: Camera Press Ltd)
With Chou En-lai (Photo: Rex Features)
An Unexpected Meeting (Photo: Keystone Press)
With President and Mrs Sadat (Photo: C. Leroy/Sipa)
With the Queen Mother (Photo: Keystone Press)
With James Callaghan (Photo: Keystone Press)

Between pages 112–113

Relaxing at the Villa Suvretta (Photo: Camera Press)
At a Self-service Restaurant (Photo: Keystone Press)
Opening an Exhibition in Turkey (Photo: Camera Press (ABC/AJANSI) London)
Inspecting a Children's Hospital (Photo: Keystone Press)
Being welcomed by Iranian Women (Photo: Popperfoto)
Arriving at the Tomb of Cyrus the Great (Photo: Keystone Press)
The Imperial Family (Photo: Camera Press (Sage) London)

Colour illustrations between pages 80–81

The Wedding (Paul Popper Ltd)
Crowned and Enthroned (Paul Popper Ltd)
After the Coronation Ceremony (Vizo Paris/Rex Features)
With Princess Farahnaz (Camera Press Ltd)

1

Should the King come…

When I was quite small, my mother often took me to the *hammam* (baths). There, women would come to wash our hair or our backs and, to keep the little children amused, always had a store of poems and songs. One of these women, as she rubbed me, would sing softly:

> *To whom shall we give this girl?*
> *No ordinary man shall she wed!*
> *Should the King come with his army, his Minister in his train,*
> *Perhaps she will not be wed . . .*

I wonder if that woman remembers cradling the child who, one day, became the wife of her King? I did not forget. All unknowing, it was a part of my future that she was crooning.

I was born in Teheran on 14 October, 1938. My father was from Azerbaijan and my mother from the province of Gilan, near the Caspian Sea. My father came from an old and well-known family, for my forbears have long served the country as governors of provinces, diplomats or religious leaders. One of them had great influence on the country—since the monarch then reigning often sought his advice. In those days, there was a close link between religion and the Court. My grandfather held a diplomatic appointment in the Netherlands, and then in Tiflis in the days of the Tsars. When my father was young, he went with my uncle to the Imperial Cadet School in St Petersburg. After the revolution of 1917, he went to Paris where he studied law and completed the course at Saint-Cyr. Afterwards, he returned to work here.

Through my father, I belong to a family of Seids, which means that I am descended from the Prophet through his grandsons, the sons of his daughter and the Iman Ali who is, for us, the Shiites, the lawful successor to Mahommet. It is disagreement over this succession which separates us from the Sunnite sect of Islam. My family name is Diba because one of my ancestors used to wear a kind of cape made of silk and 'diba' means 'silk'.

In the past, there were no family names in Iran. People had a title or were called 'son of So-and-So'. But since the accession to the throne of the present King's father, it has become obligatory to have one and that was the name chosen by my family.

My mother comes from a great family in the province of Gilan and in her family, too, the men are prominent in the religious hierarchy. When my mother was young, very little importance was attached to the intellectual education of women, but in spite of this, she went to the École Jeanne d'Arc, a Christian school in Teheran, and then completed her secondary schooling.

Despite this background, very Mohammedan, as you see, I have never worn the *tchador*, that long, dark veil in which Iranian women traditionally drape themselves. That shows how enlightened and open-minded my family were. Their faith is deep but quite free from intolerance or sectarianism.

I am, alas, an only child and longed for a brother or sister. Fortunately, ever since her marriage, my mother has lived in the same house as her brother, who had an only son, and we were brought up together rather like brother and sister. When I was born, my mother was not really too pleased that I was a girl: in Iran, people like their first child to be a boy. So the doctor told her, and these were his very words: 'Look, it is a little angel!' Well, I hope she no longer has any regrets.

Watching my character and my behaviour, and listening to what I said, members of my family would look at one another and declare: 'She is exactly like her father!'

10

Yet I certainly did not have long enough to imitate him for he died when I was nine years old and photographs make comparisons difficult because of his thick moustaches . . .

Also, I greatly resemble my mother. Sometimes, when I see a photograph of her in a paper, I feel I am looking at myself, or, if I see one of myself, it looks just like her. There are, too, striking likenesses of character: this wish to be always kind to everyone, this tendency to live for others, the inability to say things that need saying through fear of hurting others . . . They are, no doubt, good qualities, but verging on the impractical: it is living to give pleasure to others and forgetting to think of oneself. I have usually found my pleasure in that of others—now, I am trying to alter that a little because my work, with all the strain it involves, is very tiring. I shall put myself first for a change. Talking of everyday life, my husband sometimes says to me: 'You do not take decisions.' A small example? If we are going skiing, I never say which slope I would prefer, I ask the others what they would like and find more pleasure in complying with their choice than in making my own.

In Iran, family life is very close and, when I was young, there were many gatherings of cousins, aunts, uncles, great-aunts, great-uncles and so on. Since my paternal grandmother had been twice married—each time to a cousin, as custom then required—and had seven sons and two daughters, we were very numerous. In addition, I had a nurse—a nanny, as we used to say—whom I adored because, as is so often the case, she was very indulgent and much less insistent on discipline than were my parents. I was rather spoiled, the object of much kindness and affection. While my father was alive, we lived very comfortably. His parents were possibly richer than my mother's, for he came of a landed family. But I am glad he was not himself a landowner. He worked in the legal department of the army. He loved me dearly and devoted much attention to me. For instance, there were not many vaccines for children in Iran, so he had them specially sent from abroad for me. He forbade people to come into my room in dirty shoes and would not allow me to be kissed by all and sundry. Nor were there many toys. While the others played with rag dolls, I had one which said 'Papa—Mamma'. Such things seem unimportant today, but in those days it was rare and wonderful for a child to own a bicycle of the right size for his or her age.

Life, therefore, was good and I have only happy memories of my childhood. As the journalists in the Sunday papers like to put it: 'Some good fairy must have touched her cradle with a magic wand.' Certainly, it cannot be compared with the material advantages enjoyed by children today, but what matters is to be happy in the circumstances in which one finds oneself, with the possibilities one has. I might not even have asked for as much as I had, for in my circle, among my own kind, it seemed to me that I had everything I needed and I never wanted more. The only 'frustration'—a very grand word—I can recall is when, at the age of thirteen or fourteen, I felt envious of those who were going skiing. No one in my family skied and my mother would not send me to the youth clubs. Those passing cars loaded with skis were the only things I looked at with longing. But I have more than made up for it since . . .

In Teheran, we lived in a pleasant house which is still standing and which I often feel I should like to re-visit. In summer, we went to that part of the town where I live now, Shemiran. In those days, it was a suburb of Teheran, almost in the country, and much cooler because it was five hundred metres higher than the city centre. I liked the summers because the house was always full. Everyone—family, servants, guests—gathered there, quite informally, and relatives or friends turned up at all hours to spend the night. I enjoyed the bustle and always invited cousins, both boys and girls. Beds would be made up on the floor of a large living room or out in the garden under mosquito nets. I was delighted that we should spend all our time together. The days were entirely given up to games or excursions. At that time, there were very few houses at Shemiran, but many

fields, big gardens and streams. We went climbing, rode
donkeys among the hills, wandered through the valleys.
Being something of a tomboy, always climbing trees, I
preferred to play with my boy cousins. After five
minutes with the girls, playing dolls, I would be bored
and go off cycling with the boys.

Life was very different then. More primitive, perhaps,
but sometimes more beautiful. The houses had no running water and drinking water was brought round in
horse-drawn carts. There was a certain charm about the
man with his buckets and his cry: 'The water-carrier is
here . . .' The door would be opened to him, he would fill
the pitchers and all the other containers. Water for washing ourselves and for the little pool was drawn from the
stream across the road. It was very dirty but I remember
that the moment when it poured into the pool was one of
great excitement for the children. For the grown-ups,
too. Each district was allotted a special day for drawing
this water and everyone tried to be first to fill his reser-
voirs. There were arguments between the houses about
the setting of the little weir or the removing of a neigh-
bour's to channel the water into one's own house first.
On the water floated lots of orange skins or old shoes. . . .

Teheran was only a small town. None of the northern
districts, where the great reinforced concrete hotels
stand now, existed then. It was still meadowland,
nothing else. People went there for picnics, to gather
herbs for the kitchen, to enjoy themselves and felt almost
as if they had gone on a short excursion. No one thought
the town would spread as it has and become one of the
largest in the world.

I used to love playing in the street with my small
neighbours. My parents forbade it but as soon as their
backs were turned, we would go out and sit beside the
door to watch the people go by, or play a fierce game of
volley-ball in the roadway. Few, indeed, were the cars to
interrupt us. Sometimes, the ice-cream van would
appear and be immediately besieged by a horde of children. Its delights were probably not very hygienic and
my parents, if they had known, would have scolded

us—this, needless to say, doubled our pleasure!

The Iran of those days was picturesque because of this street life and it would be a great pity if it should entirely disappear. Pedlars cried their wares in song and their offerings marked the changing seasons: in winter, there were beetroots; in spring, there would be trays of fresh vegetables, with radishes and mint which the Iranians add to everything; then would come the first fruits: the first strawberries, the first oranges, the first cucumbers. Each trader described his wares in song and each vegetable had its special tune—quite a repertory. In summer, people drove out to Shemiran to eat roasted corn and kebabs. There, our water pitchers would be filled from leather bottles made of sheepskin. For the radiator of the car, we used a hand-pump; it was the great joy of the children to take it in turn to prove their strength. Sometimes, a piece of cloth had to be wrapped around the tap, to keep out the small animals swimming about in the water.

At the time, our house, the garden, the courtyard and the pool which adorned it all seemed to me very big. Now that I am grown-up, they would undoubtedly look quite different. When I sometimes return to places I knew as a child, I am always astonished to find them so small. The garden was filled with flowers, especially roses—the full-blown, highly-scented roses which reach their full bloom only in the country of Hafez and Saadi. In summer in the little kitchen garden shaded by the Japonica, grew mint and green peppers. In a corner, were a few pigeons and some sheep.

I have always liked dogs: as a little girl, I used to collect them in the street and take them home. My mother would keep them for a while, then give them away or chase them off. She considered them dirty. This upset me and I would be very angry with her. When my father was alive, we had a big dog called Tchorni which, in Russian, means 'black'. My mother lost him but he walked for days and days and eventually found his way back to the house. I shall never forget that.

Downstairs was the private sitting-room. I used to

sleep in the same room as my parents and whenever they went out in the evening, I always found sweets, chocolates and goodies under my pillow the next morning. On the first floor was my father's study, the big dining-room and the reception rooms. On the far side of the garden was a garage, for we had a car. The servants were people who had known our family for a long time and I was very fond of them. I always wanted to be with them and so, as soon as my parents went out, my cousin and I would go to their room, sit on their knee and they would tell us stories.

My earliest memories centre around this house of my childhood for, after my father's death, life became more difficult and we had to move.

It is strange, but my mother always kept from me the fact of my father's death. Nowadays, it is different. Children are told the truth, but she must have thought it would cause me great grief for I was, it seems, very, very devoted to him. But I guessed the truth from overhearing the servants or members of the family. No sooner did someone mention him than everyone would say 'Hush'. I realised something was wrong and felt hurt. 'Why does my mother keep it from me?' I wondered. Strangest of all, I never spoke to my mother about my father until the day I left for Paris to continue my studies, in other words, from the age of nine until I was seventeen! At first, I was told he had gone to Europe for medical treatment, and I believed this. It was even a source of some pride to me for, in those days, it was fairly unusual. But, before very long, in only a few weeks' time, I realised, when questioning my mother as she played with me, that Father was dead. She had told me that the man who had died was a great-uncle in the family and I asked her: 'If he is everyone's uncle, why is it that you are sadder than the others? Why does my father not write to us?' She replied that he was ill and I said: 'Other people are ill but they write.' We never spoke of it again. We had to leave that house and live in an apartment. In material ways, life was harder. And then, little by little, it became more comfortable, thanks to the position my uncle had found.

We moved to one house, then another and finally to that to which I returned after my two years of study in Paris.

My mother, naturally, went through a difficult time. She had to bring me up alone, to be both father and mother. In Iran everyone sets great store by what other people think: 'What will the family say?'—'What will everyone say?' and Mother was quite strict with me in the matters of my studies, my manners, my friends, about going out—about everything. For example, she was terribly upset when I had to re-take my dictation examination in the third form. I must have been eleven, and my mark was zero. She made a terrible fuss, as if I had brought some dishonour on the family. It was quite incredible! I felt I had committed the most heinous of faults, that I was a dreadfully ungrateful child. I wept so much that my eyes swelled until I could not open them. My mother kept it secret from her nearest kin as if it were shameful . . .

Yes, she was strict but perhaps, after all, she was right to be so for she was always sensible enough to understand my needs at various ages. She let me go scouting, although it was mixed, and on journeys or picnics organised by the school. Today, such things are accepted as normal, but in those days they were less commonplace. I learned to swim in a public swimming-pool and there were members of the family who said: 'But that is not done! You are sending your daughter with the boys!' Mother also allowed me to do various sports. All this constituted the pattern of my youth. It is to her that I owe all this and I thank her, because others were not allowed to do these things.

Mother sent me to Paris to study at a time when it was unusual to find a young Iranian girl there alone. And even though she knew that I would not be entirely on my own, such a decision did, after all, take considerable understanding and also, I think, a measure of trust in me and my judgment.

I also had permission to go out with a certain group of chosen boys, but she did not like me to mix with any others. At sixteen or seventeen, when I was invited to

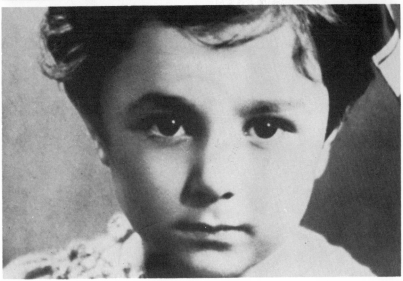

Childhood. *Above:* with cousin Reza Ghotbi, now head of
Iranian Television

The student in Paris. *Above* in the Luxembourg Gardens and
below, at the School of Architecture, 1958

Opposite the wedding,
21 December 1959.
Above happy and poised
immediately after the
ceremony and *below,*
freeing doves as a token
of happiness and peace

Above taking part in the
annual Scout Festival.
Right with the Shah and
their ten months' old son,
September 1961

Opposite on holiday. *Above* at Bosolsar, Caspian Sea, in 1962.
Below, the Imperial Family at the Villa Suvretta, St Moritz, February 1973

A favourite sport

Speaking after receiving an Honorary Doctorate of Philosophy from the Charles University, Prague, 1977

Honoured by *l'Académie des Beaux Arts*, Paris, 1974

parties where there was dancing, I was usually allowed to go, depending on where it was, but I always had to return home at a set time, escorted by my friends' parents.

It is certain that my mother must sometimes have found it difficult to make ends meet. But the pocket money she gave me—even if others were given more—always seemed to me sufficient. At the end of each month, I always managed to buy whatever I wanted: bits and pieces that I needed for school, also magazines, newspapers, records, treats for my girl friends and myself. I never went without—thanks, perhaps, to the affection of my family. At one time, we did not have many pairs of shoes or dresses but this meant that if we were given a dress for New Year or our birthday, it was a wonderful event. It is a part of our New Year tradition always to wear something new that day. If it is impossible to have an entirely new outfit, one must wear at least a new pair of stockings. So our comparative lack of means only enhanced these occasions. All these joys were a part of the charm of living. Looking forward to presents was almost a rite.

It taught me to always try to deserve what I had. I bought my first bicycle with presents of money given me for the New Year. I put it all together for that purpose, and how I looked after that bicycle—cleaning it and taking the greatest possible care of it. In those days, cycling in the streets held few dangers. I also remember my first white balloon, so dear to my heart. Balloons, too, were rare. And then, my first elasticated bathing dress. These were completely novel to us, since we only had swimming costumes made of cloth, or wool, none of which were very pretty nor did they fit very well. But when someone wanted to give this to me, I said: 'Wait until I learn to swim, and then . . .' To deserve it, to earn it, that doubled my pleasure. Taking all in all, I was, I think, well dressed and never envied anyone. In the circle in which I lived, I felt at ease.

Like other girls of good family, my mother wanted to send me to ballet lessons, but because of a chill, I believe,

17

that had to be abandoned. I had my first piano lessons when I was five, but as we did not have a piano in the house, I had to practise at school, where the instrument stood always in the darkest places. I was truly afraid to stay behind after school to practise and that is why I was not a very diligent pupil. Later, when my mother bought a piano, I disliked being alone in the big drawing-room and always insisted on the company of a servant who would have to invent some reason for staying with me while I practised my scales. It was not until my Paris days that I began to study interesting music. Then, I began to play for my own pleasure. Previously it had been in obedience to my mother.

When I was a child, the only means in Iran of obtaining a proper education and preparing for slightly more advanced studies, was to attend the western schools. That is why, when I was quite small, my parents, who wanted me to learn a foreign language, entered me for the Italian School in Teheran. It was run by Italian nuns and the teaching was in both Persian and French. I still remember my first day there. I was terribly nervous and huddled into a corner. I wore a red tartan skirt—not very becoming, because the nuns would not allow short skirts—and carried a small satchel in which I had an apple and a blue note-book. I was so timid that if the other girls asked me for the biscuits or sandwiches I had brought for the ten o'clock 'break', I would hand them over without a word. I stayed four years at this school.

Afterwards, I spent five years at the École Jeanne d'Arc, which was also run by nuns. I thoroughly enjoyed these years because of all the sport. I was very keen on sport and excelled at it. I played basket-ball and took part in athletics, running and jumping. In those days, there were not many teams in Iran and we used to win all the competitions and carry off all the medals. As I was Captain of the team, victories brought honour and a triumphal return. I earned the admiration of the school and was included in the pupils' gallery of sporting heroes which, I think, accounted for my popularity. Children would even point me out to their parents:

'There she is!' And the teachers were nicer to me because I won cups for the school. If, now and then, I did not know my lesson, they were more lenient towards me than they would otherwise have been.

The school also used to arrange picnics and games outside the city, scientific visits to different factories and journeys into the provinces. Our cultural visit to Ispahan was a particularly happy one because, for the first time, the girls from Jeanne d'Arc and the boys from Saint-Louis—the school run by the French priests—joined forces. These two schools were the oldest in Teheran. They are now more than one hundred years old. There were also festivals of sport with rhythmic gymnastics, and fancy-dress balls. I went to one of these dressed as Prince Charming.

It was often thought that those who attended these schools were more or less persuaded by the nuns to adopt the Christian religion. I, myself, liked going to church. I liked the atmosphere, the hymns, the candles: it was pretty. But I was given a Moslem education by my own family, who were very devout, and being present at the Catholic Mass never influenced me, even for a moment. Already, I felt we could each pray to our own God no matter where we were, that God is the same everywhere and that what is important is to pray to him without sectarianism or intolerance. And even if some young Iranian girls did become Christian, I do not recall the nuns ever attempting proselytism.

The École Jeanne d'Arc had an atmosphere all of its own. We always try to remember only the pleasant things, but how could one forget those great refectories where lunch was brought to us in tin bowls and re-heated. With our little uniforms—black overalls with white collars—it was like some scene from *Oliver Twist* and the dark basement rooms were rather frightening. In summer, there was often a shortage of water and we would be thirsty. Indeed, we were far from having the facilities enjoyed by schoolchildren today . . .

It was at Jeanne d'Arc that I began the most enriching adventure of my youth: scouting. The more so as I was neither a scout nor a guide, but a cub mistress. This helped to teach me a sense of responsibility and to cultivate in me a taste for simplicity in personal relationships. The programme and the uniform were those of the French Scouts and there were a few young French boys among us. But the entire organisation remained Iranian and it was, for instance, the army which provided the lorries for transporting the children. Summer camps, comradeship, camp fires, resourcefulness, it was all as wholesome as it was enjoyable and I often saw my cousin, who was also a scout.

It was through scouting that I made my first acquaintance with France. A few of us, two girls and two boys, organised an entertainment in a theatre and with the money from the sale of tickets, we set out for Paris in the summer of 1956. We knew we could rely on the hospitality of families with children in the scout movement. I spent a few days in a family where the son was a scout and the daughter a cub mistress.

It was our first visit to Paris. As soon as we arrived, we walked to the Étoile and then set out to look for the other historic buildings of which we had seen pictures. Afterwards, we left with a group for Jambville—an extraordinary property, an old château with a huge garden, not far from Paris, which belongs to the Scouts of France. There, we found young people from all over the world. Each group took it in turn to present their national life, to sing traditional songs and to improvise an entertainment based on their country's folk-lore. There was something very moving in this genuine and unbiased interchange—a warm, sincere friendship between children of all nations. It was splendid and I wish that, as grownups, we could have remained as little aware as we were then of the frontiers which separate us. Jambville was what is known as a Drama Camp and here we learned to mime, act, produce plays, speak to very young children, read or recite poems and to write a few paragraphs each evening when we got home.

Next, we went to a place near Royan to set up our tents beside the sea for a Physical Education Camp. Our aim was to learn to organise the sporting activities of our wolf-cubs. This time, it was all much more technical—how many minutes for this movement or that . . . On one occasion, I had to go off alone into the countryside for the whole day, taking just three matches. I had to be able to follow a trail, to prepare a light lunch from my handful of provisions, to bring back certain plants, perhaps even a few small creatures. It was very exciting. The countryside, the small French villages are quite different from ours and we laid in there a stock of radiant good health which would certainly stand us in good stead later. I do not know what became of most of the French boys and girls at the camp. I was sad to learn that one of them had been killed in Algeria.

I often think of those wolf-cubs, who are now grown men. Of those in my pack, one now works in the Palace in the children's school and another has become my dentist.

At home, family holidays were spent beside the Caspian, paddling in the sea from morning till night, or else in Azerbaijan, on a property belonging to relatives. There, mingling with the peasants, we led a farm life. We learned to pick rice or tea and, knowing that the women workers were paid according to the number of kilos they brought home each evening, we helped with the harvesting by filling the baskets of the oldest among them so that they could earn more money. We went riding or sat with the peasants, opening water-melons with sickles. To us children, it was a great treat to go into the gardens and gorge on fruits until we were sick. Sometimes we went on pilgrimage, to spend a little time in quiet meditation in the holy places of our faith.

After passing my Lower Certificate examination, I left the École Jeanne d'Arc to spend the last three years of my secondary studies in the Lycée Razi, a Franco-Persian lay establishment. Today, it is a big lycée with more than three thousand five hundred pupils, but in my day it was quite small, to the south of the town, and we were few in number. In the Baccalauréat year we were perhaps fewer than twenty. Unfortunately, the buildings have now disappeared. They were pulled down and I am very sad about it. I should have insisted that they be preserved. I did not do so because I did not want it thought that I was saying: 'Keep them because of me' when my real thought was 'Keep them as an example of a school of that period'. It was an old house. The classes were held in tiled, semi-basement rooms with columns and the teacher would enter through the window. The setting was very attractive, as picturesque as it was decrepit, even to the extent that the irrigation channels in the garden would sometimes crumble and flood all the classrooms. The pieces of furniture were all equally shaky and in the laboratory, which was used occasionally, nothing worked. It was covered in dust and not a single piece of apparatus was serviceable. You can imagine what the experiments in physics and chemistry were like. The cupboards were full of geological specimens, all with the wrong labels. In our scorn, we used to draw derisory little caricatures. The atmosphere was warm and friendly, for the children, all from the same schools, had known one another all their lives. Because we were so few, there was very close contact between teachers, pupils and servants. The quality of the education was exceptional. All those who went through this lycée did brilliantly well in their studies and are now professors or even rectors of universities, doctors, senior officials. In short, they occupy all the leading posts.

I was one of three girls who were inseparable—we were known as the Three Musketeers—and every morning we would take the bus or a taxi together to the lycée. We lunched there, for it was a long way from our homes, and took it in turn to bring the meal for all of us, eating it hungrily together. There was, in fact, neither canteen nor cafeteria and all we could buy on the spot was ordinary bread.

I have the happiest memories of those days. There were many escapades, but harmless ones. We were not difficult pupils and our fun always remained within acceptable limits. Things have changed enormously since then and the young of today have quite a different outlook. We were sometimes punished, of course, but we never did anything serious. I myself was very serious-minded and very hard-working. I joined in all the escapades but always managed not to be caught. I was the sort of pupil for whom teachers have a regard and whom they are apt to quote as examples. But I was much less earnest than I appeared. I studied hard but took part in all that was going on. I was involved in all the mischief, but without attracting attention. On those occasions when I *was* punished, there was general surprise. The Iranian teachers taught in French, but we spoke the language better than they did. They had the most extraordinary accents and turns of phrase. One day, I could not help laughing and was sent out of the room. As it was the first time, everyone exclaimed: 'That's a change!'

I had many friends among the girls at the Lycée Razi. Since those days, the circle of my close friends has grown smaller but the three or four companions who were closest to me then have remained so. Their friendship is still very important to me, especially now. I have known them for twenty-seven years, we attended the same classes, sat on the same benches and I like to keep in touch with them because I know they are true friends since our friendship dates from before I became Queen. Of those I have met since then, it is always possible to wonder: 'Are they my friends or is it because of my position that they are so kind?' Of course, other women have become real friends since then, but it is the group of those made before my marriage that I see most frequently. Besides, some of them work in the organisations over which I preside, or in the universities. I meet them, therefore, in the course of my duties as well as during the holidays, when they always come with me, together with their husbands and their children. Now that my husband's family know them well, we are always together and they often say jokingly: 'We are some of these chattels mentioned in your marriage contract!'

What was I reading all this time? A little of everything,

some very bad, some very good. When I was quite small and did not know how to read, I used to enjoy looking at the pictures in all the illustrated magazines—not very good literature for children. Later, the books we were given at school were the most innocent of romantic novels, which we loved, or else adventure stories and the illustrated papers of the day: *The Intrepid* or *Brave Souls*. In those days there was very little interesting reading matter for children. Afterwards came the cloyingly sentimental magazines and then every kind of romantic love-story, like those of Delly, Max du Veuzit and others.

Then we plunged into the thrillers and cloak-and-dagger novels, coming eventually to Saint-Exupéry, Maxence van der Meersch and Camus. Later, of course, I grew to love such French poets as Eluard, Prévert, Aragon or Baudelaire. In short, a very typical progression. At the Lycée Razi, French literature was taught very intelligently: we read Racine aloud, each of us taking a part and trying to give the words the appropriate intonation. It was not a question of learning by heart but of understanding all these great writers.

At the same time, there was growing within me this love of the arts which governed a part of my life. Is it hereditary? I do not know but there is no doubt that I owe it to my family. My grandfather, a well-informed amateur, was a dedicated collector of Iranian works of art. In Tiflis, he had studied the books and Iranian works in the Russian museums and every day he would illustrate with little drawings the personal journal he kept in Russian. After him, my father carried on this work. He was a gifted caricaturist and I think it is from him that I inherit the modest talent I have for drawing and music.

Politics we followed only from a great distance. I was not quite three years old when my future husband ascended the throne. But I was ten at the time of the first attempt to assassinate him, which was in 1948. We were all very frightened. My family was deeply royalist and had great admiration and respect for the King. I was at my aunt's when I heard of the attack and she was immediately terrified at the thought of what might happen. But, without delay, the King spoke to his people on the radio. We knew that he was safe and all the fears were allayed. But it was indeed a miracle that he escaped with his life. The assassin was three metres away from him when he fired. The first three bullets went through his helmet, grazing his head. Suddenly, he felt quite alone, there was no longer anyone near him. Instinctively, everyone had fled or hidden. Then the King had the courage to face his assailant and try to dodge the bullets. The fourth grazed his shoulder blade—the scar is still faintly visible—the fifth went through his lip and the sixth did not fire. God was with him.

I also remember—it was in 1950—the return of the ashes of Reza Shah, my husband's father, who had died in exile in Johannesburg. The King was in the procession and it was always a great event when he appeared in public. People would wait for hours in the street to catch a glimpse of him. I always went, and so had seen him before, on his return from Azerbaijan after its reconquest. He was given a hero's welcome and received in triumph. The enthusiasm was unbelievable. Every time I saw the King, I would weep with emotion.

I have another happy memory of Azerbaijan, a typically Iranian story: when I returned there, a groom proudly presented me with the mare on which one of my relatives had fought the rebels. The poor animal was scarcely capable of putting one foot before the other, but she was still cared for with tremendous respect because she had fought in the campaign . . .

Afterwards, we went through some very difficult times. In 1951, General Razmara, our Prime Minister, was assassinated. At school this made a deep impression on us and we were very upset because his daughter was one of our school companions. Then, there was a wave of attacks and assassinations. A most unpleasant atmosphere was abroad in the land. It was the beginning of the Mossadegh period. Personally, I have never been pro-Mossadegh, though I did feel proud when he nationalised oil. But it caused the Government serious financial

25

problems. State bonds were sold to everyone so that each individual should help to pay off the deficit. They were even on sale in the École Jeanne d'Arc and we all bought them. Politics came into everything. In family life, there was no longer respect for fathers, great-uncles or great-aunts. Some were in favour of the policies, others against and there were arguments and counter-arguments. At home, one day, I heard a terrible argument between my cousin, who was fifteen or sixteen, and a great-uncle who must have been fifty—they were hurling insults at one another like a couple of street urchins! And then the schools organised expeditions to fight one another, sometimes with knives. It usually ended in a pitched battle. Even girls, or children from the primary schools took part in the general disorder. Communist newspapers were sold in the town, quarrels tore everyone apart, from the simplest to the most sophisticated. My cousin, who was a royalist, stopped the young communists organising strikes in the schools and destroyed their newspapers. One day, he was knifed in the back but, luckily, the wound was not very deep. He was one of those who, when the King decided to go, went to demonstrate in front of the palace to prevent him leaving us. Naturally, my uncle was terribly worried at having a young son involved in politics, because some were arrested by the police. There were telephone calls in the evenings with such news as 'So-and-So has been arrested' . . .

It all made a deep impression on me. All these demonstrations, disorders, bombs, shots, tanks and tear gas worried me so much that I could not eat. When the King left, we were staying on the shores of the Caspian Sea in a boarding-house where there was a Russian refugee woman who scared me by saying: 'It is exactly like the revolution of 1917!' Indeed, we did wonder what would happen, for there was certainly a similarity in the situation. After the King's departure, people went around for two or three days breaking statues, changing the name of everything called Pahlavi and destroying official portraits. And then, suddenly, from one day to the next

—overnight—all was reversed and there was a wild royalist enthusiasm.

At the time, I did not think very deeply about the significance of these events. I was too busy feeling relief that everything had been settled. Later, I understood just how volatile the public can be if it is neither sufficiently well-informed in political matters nor master of its opinions. It is capable of a sudden about-turn. Of course, the great majority of the people was behind the King and that is why there arose this spontaneous movement to demand his return. But it had not stopped people from going to extremes.

I had always wanted to continue my studies in France. Besides, it was quite straightforward since our Baccalauréat at the Lycée Razi was recognised by the French universities. My first idea was to become a laboratory assistant because I liked working with microscopes. Luckily, I did not choose that path. I could never have lived shut in from morning till night in the same small room. But my uncle was an architect and my cousin, whom I liked very much, was at the School of Architecture in Paris. So, as I was good at mathematics and drawing, and liked the idea of creating new buildings, of working out-of-doors, I wrote to this cousin, asking him to tell me something about it. In the end, I was admitted to the same School of Architecture.

It must be said that, at this time, the range of possible careers was not very great. Choice was very limited. We did not know what it would be possible to do; we concentrated on what it would be possible to study and hoped to be able to find a good job later. For this reason, most of the students were headed towards the professions of engineering, medicine or architecture. Alternatively, being gifted at the piano, I could equally well have tried to enter the Conservatory of Music to become a pianist. But I am increasingly convinced now that I chose my career well, for I am still deeply interested in everything to do with building, architecture and town-planning.

I had applied for a scholarship and could reasonably

27

hope to get one as I had passed first in the Baccalauréat. I went, therefore, to the Ministry of Education. It was my first contact with Iranian bureaucracy, and not a very happy one because none of the officials knew exactly what procedure should be followed. I was told I had to pass an examination in languages or other subjects in order to qualify for a scholarship. But no one knew the date of this examination, not even the Minister of Education, whom I had had an opportunity of meeting.

The days and the weeks went by. In Paris, the School had already opened and there was I, wandering from one office to another, from one person to another, receiving only such answers as: 'Today. Tomorrow. The day after tomorrow. No one knows. Wait . . .' I was so angry that I said: 'I am leaving and shall never return. I shall just manage as best I can'. I fumed at the idea of all the days of term these people were making me lose. In the end, since they could not make up their minds, I left without waiting for their scholarship, as my mother was in a position to send me some money. It was quite enough for me to manage on, particularly since I was able to live in the cité universitaire, which was much less expensive than taking a room in town. It was not easy to obtain a place there, many forms had to be filled in, many letters written, but I was helped a little by our relatives in Paris.

In this 'University Centre', I found the surroundings really pleasant, a very comfortable life compared with that of some students lost in a strange city in conditions that were sometimes difficult and depressing. I remember going to visit friends in dark rooms at the end of long, dark corridors, in attics, icy in winter and stifling in summer, without water, a cracked hand basin on the stairs, five storeys to climb on foot and so much noise: television, football matches, the loud voices of neighbours. It was depressing. The cité universitaire is a very pleasant place. The gardens were splendid in the spring with all their flowers and the food in the restaurant was delicious. I was always able, with whatever money I had, to manage to live well. I could pay my rent, the tuition fees, the season ticket on the Métro and the food tickets, which were the essentials. And if, after paying for these things, I had to buy any rather expensive materials for my course, or to travel, my mother would kindly send me a little extra.

I lived in the Netherlands Pavilion, which was considered the most serious-minded. The Director was M. Merkus and we were always known as 'M. Merkus' girls'. Boys and girls were not allowed to visit one another's rooms, except sometimes during the day for just a few minutes, so it became a kind of sport for the boys to try to get into the girls' section, wearing wigs to make them look like young ladies, merely to annoy the staff. Every year we kept the Dutch custom of celebrating the feast of St Nicholas with a gay party.

The house was not very luxurious and the linoleum along the corridors gave it a homely appearance, but the building was modern and light. I had a room on the third floor overlooking the avenue which leads at right angles off the Boulevard Jourdan, near the Porte d'Orléans. A hand-basin hidden in a cupboard, a brown desk of hardboard beside the window with drawers and shelves for books, a table, an armchair, a little wooden bed, that was all. I decorated the walls with photographs of the family or friends, drawings I had made in the studio or posters which I used to bring back from my travels. We were not allowed to use drawing-pins, so they were stuck up with Scotch tape. I had inherited from my cousin a very ancient but very precious gramophone. Such was my passion for music that I remember listening one day for an hour and a half on the telephone to a recording I loved, played for me by a girl-friend at the other end of the line. My cousin and I bought the 78-rpm records being sold in the streets—those of Caruso, for instance, which the hawkers used to display on the pavements. And I always listened to the programmes of classical music on the radio. My friends and I would often discuss them and there grew between us a sort of rivalry in musical knowledge.

In winter, it was so cold because of the metal-framed

windows that, in order to study, I had to wrap myself in a 'poustine', a sort of Iranian waistcoat of sheepskin, the fleece being on the inside, which Afghanistan has made so fashionable today, and pile on several pairs of stockings. It was impossible even to plug in a radiator because it would blow the fuses! The only comfort was the communal shower-room and a place where we washed and ironed our clothes.

Breakfasts were served in the Pavilion and except when we were organising celebrations or parties, we would take our meals in the Centre's restaurant. But sometimes, and naturally without permission, we would secretly prepare little Iranian dishes in my room on a small spirit stove. For *Nowrouz*, our New Year, which is kept on the twenty-first of March, I used things my mother had sent me to prepare in miniature and set around my room in the traditional manner the seven elements whose Persian names begin with 's'. For us, they all symbolise plenty and joy.

But my life in Paris was not always easy. I was, doubtless, rather romantic and sentimental. The first year was very difficult for me, despite my good knowledge of French. The course was very hard because I had specialised in the natural sciences and entry to the School of Architecture normally required a Baccalauréat in mathematics. I found the mathematics very uphill work. As for descriptive geometry, it was a nightmare. And, for the first time, I was meeting the challenge of competition.

At university, people naturally choose subjects in which they consider themselves most talented, so competition becomes increasingly stiff, and I, who had been a good student in Iran, did not feel quite at home in such a different setting. In Teheran, we were a group of fifteen or sixteen friends who had known one another for years. Suddenly, I found myself dealing with a different mentality, dominated by the spirit of competition, which is far from pleasant, since it means that the less well you do yourself, the more opportunity you give to others. No one tries to help you, even a little. During the examination, if someone bemoaned the fact that ink had been upset over the plan on which he was working, all the others would say: 'Good, that means one less!'

There was another difference: the freshman tradition which, in the schools of medicine and even more in those of art, means that the older students rag the newcomers and set them to do all kinds of humiliating tasks. True, the School of Architecture was less tough than the School of Fine Arts, and it was the boys who suffered most from the ragging. A measure of pity was shown the girls. As for me, I arrived two weeks after the beginning of term and so fortunately escaped the worst of the ragging. It may be that such unkindnesses help to form character, if one is strong enough to withstand them, but for some foreigners, rather at sea and far from home, it is sometimes so hard that they prefer to return to their own country.

The bawdy songs they loved to sing in those schools were for me, an Iranian girl of the old fashioned kind, terribly shocking. To enter the studios, we had to knock on the door, wait for permission from the seniors and say: 'Thank you, most noble and venerable seniors!' Sometimes, they would make us climb on the table, dance, sing and talk in every tongue. If we grumbled or lost our tempers, they would give us a 'jar', which meant having to open one's mouth and say 'Ah, Ah' while a glass of water was thrown in one's face. If anyone resisted, there would be more glasses of water, but if you laughed, they did not know how to deal with it. In this, too, I managed quite well and did not have too many misfortunes.

The poor boys were told to stand naked on a table. We did not dare lift our eyes. We were sent to other studios to fetch things which did not exist, such as spiral compasses' and everyone laughed at us. I stood in great fear of being sent to another studio for we were always obliged to kiss one of the bearded students. We had to do everything the seniors wanted us to do, to carry their drawing-boards like some servant . . . They stole our instruments, the T-squares, the set squares, the compasses. It was forbidden to ask for them back or to have, as they did, padlocks on our drawers. We had to draw incredible things and then, if we grew angry, it made things worse, if we gave any hint of shyness, it was worse still, and if we looked aggressive, that was worst of all.

I was homesick the first year and did not expect to return to Iran for four or five years, even during the holidays. (In fact, I only stayed two years in Paris.) So I was often sad, and felt lonely and miserable. Besides, I found everything so depressing: as I left very early in the morning, I used to see the workmen, young and old, struggling off to work in the Métro and I felt sorry for them, I suffered for them and for those old women wandering aimlessly along the corridors, a cigarette drooping from a corner of their mouth. I had, alas, plenty of time to watch them, for I took private lessons in descriptive geometry from a professor living at the Porte de Saint-Ouen, which is at almost exactly the opposite end of Paris from the Porte d'Orléans. From Métro to Métro, it took me two hours to get there and back, nearly always standing, for the second class was often packed. None of this brought any comfort. I spent much of my time in my room drinking tea, alone with the memory of what I had seen. Even the films we watched were anything but gay since it was not 'done' to go to the cinema for amusement. Students were supposed to see serious films and we came out weighed down with tragedy. The attitude to books was the same.

The second year was much easier. When first entering a new community, it can be difficult to understand its members, their manner of speaking, dressing, behaving. It is impossible to distinguish fellow-spirits, those with whom one would get on well. Later, one makes friends, learns to explore and discover favourite haunts, to recognise one's own kind and way of life. Also, I had myself become a senior, the situation was reversed and now it was my turn to make others do things, not unkind ones, of course, but I did at last have some standing. No one might touch my stool, my name was written on it; I

had a padlock for my drawer and I had my heavy drawing boards carried by a freshman. And, of course, he had
to say he enjoyed it all and wished with all his heart it
could last—otherwise, the 'jar'!

In drawing, I had few problems, for I was quite
talented. But to start with, I found it difficult to repro-
duce the models. At first, they were Greek or Roman
statues: Venus, Michaelangelo's Slave, the Discobolus
and, later, live models. The professor told me: 'You
Orientals know nothing about perspective because in
your miniatures everything is on the same plane.' And
my marks were not good. But I worked so hard at it that
there came a day when my drawing was put up in the
studio. That was a great honour. There was much rejoicing, I stood my friends drinks and since then have continued to draw well. In every field, it is necessary to
persevere to achieve results.

Once a year, each of the studios in the School of
Architecture gave a fancy-dress dinner. That day, the
students could say and do whatever they liked to the
professors. In theory, there was complete freedom. But
we naturally feared that, if we were too malicious, they
would later be revenged. We criticised them a little, in
fun, we told them how we felt, but it was all very mild.
On one of these occasions, the theme was 'Ancient
Rome' and we all draped ourselves in different lengths of
cloth, in curtains or bedcovers: fantasy ran riot.

But beyond these few celebrations at the School or the
cité universitaire, I never had time for amusement. The
School of Architecture was rather like a prolongation of
secondary school: I did not feel at all like a real student,
who attends two hours of lectures here, three hours
there, with a free half-day in between. I was tied to the
School from nine o'clock in the morning until five o'clock
in the afternoon. We had to sign on when we arrived and
remain in the school until evening, which did not leave
us much free time, especially since, after classes, there
was further study to be done, plans to be prepared or
calculations.

Most of my life in Paris was spent between the

Boulevard Jourdan and the Boulevard Raspail. Of course, I explored Paris to look at and study the various monuments and to make surveys. And of course I went for walks: the Boulevard Saint-Michel or the Boulevard Saint-Germain, the gardens of the Luxembourg, the Bois de Boulogne sometimes, to take out a boat or to lunch in a restaurant. Members of my family came from time to time to take me to the cinema. The first time I saw the Champs-Elysées, it was at night and it seemed another world.

But I did not spend the whole of those two years in Paris itself. During the holidays, I went on short journeys. First of all, to Spain. A group of us went to stay for a while with a Spanish girl-friend, to visit Bilbâo, Saint-Sebastian, Toledo. To enter the churches, one had to wear a mantilla—I looked just like an Andalusian. In January 1959, during the winter holidays, we arranged with two or three Iranians working in different parts of Europe, to meet in Munich at the house of a friend who was studying there and who is now head-mistress of my children's school. It was very amusing to compare experiences.

On the return journey, disaster befell me! In the overcrowded train, my plastic suitcase, wedged against a radiator, melted. All the instruments needed in architecture—set squares, boxes of compasses—which I had bought in Germany because they were cheaper there than in France, were burned or deformed. On another occasion, there was a visit with a group of students to the International Exhibition in Brussels. In the neighbourhood of the Atomium, a cosmopolitan atmosphere could be guaranteed and the cost was not excessive, perhaps fifty dollars for a week. One summer, we went to the Île de Batz, a tiny island off the coast of Britanny. I was delighted to be beside the sea once more, even if it bore very little resemblance to the Caspian.

At ordinary times, concerts were our main recreation. I belonged to the *Jeunesses Musicales* and went to the Opera. Other outings were more rare: to the theatre or the cinema, a few gatherings of friends, usually Iranian. I knew many of them, students, members of the Franco-Iranian Association or the Embassy and even relatives, including the cousin who had been brought up with me as a brother and has since become Director of our National Television. Sometimes, to break the monotony of university meals, we would go to slightly more elegant places. One day, I was returning with a group of friends from the Bois de Boulogne when we decided to look for a 'good little restaurant which does not charge too much' as they say in Paris. And by walking on and on—'No, that one is no good. Nor is that . . .'—we eventually landed up, I know not how, at Prunier's on the Avénue Victor-Hugo. It was a sumptuous meal, but when the bill came, we did not have enough money to settle it. We had to stay on at the table while one of us went to get some more. I thought the Maître d'Hôtel looked at us with some suspicion. We were not sure whether to laugh or to blush . . . .

Scouting, the mixed lycée, holidays with my boy cousins, all had given me an easy manner in the company of boys. I was not one of those cloistered girls suddenly parachuted into the world. In the studio, where we were only seven or eight girls among about fifty students, I got on very well with my companions. But, given my upbringing, it would not even have occurred to me to have any special boy friend with whom I would have gone out exclusively. Some of my companions did, of course, invite me to the cinema or to go dancing somewhere, but I never accepted if we were to go alone, only if there were to be others in the party. French boys naturally found this odd. I tried to explain to them: 'You are very nice, but I am not allowed to do that.' And if they persisted, if they pretended not to understand, then I would make sure they left me alone by telling them I had a fiancé in Iran.

But the truth was that I thought of marriage only as some distant and rather vague possibility. In my dreams, I hoped to find a husband whom I would be able to respect. I did not want a man I could dominate, someone unremarkable. It had to be someone of whom I could be proud, someone who shone both in intelligence and in his work. I wanted him to be very tall and, above all, fair, with green eyes. I have always found green eyes attractive. In Iran there are so many men with dark hair and dark eyes. I imagined him neither too frivolous nor too serious. I hoped that, like me, he would enjoy sport, like art and music, that he would be intelligent, kind and never dull.

In the meantime, it was my studies in Paris that were important. I did not intend to marry before they were completed. Besides, my upbringing had not led me to expect to choose my own husband. Iranian girls in those days did not have much say in such matters. They had to wait until someone came to ask their hand in marriage and had only the right to reply yes or no. My mother never spoke of it for she, too, hoped I would first of all obtain my diploma. Yet I never expected to lead an ordinary life. I was sure something exceptional would befall me—but not to the extent that it did!

To me, the King was almost a mythical person. I loved him because my family had always taught that he should be loved. I admired him because some of my uncles had fought for him in Azerbaijan and I was always told the story of those days with fervour. I also admired Soraya for her beauty—as in all Iranian families, her portrait always hung in our home beside that of the King—and I was sad when they had to separate because she could not bear children. I remember writing it in my diary: 'The King has divorced the Queen and it is a pity . . .' But I would not have understood it if the King, like Edward VIII, had abdicated for love. Who could have taken his place? Besides, he cannot have thought of doing so, even for a moment. In his case, duty overrides every other consideration.

Some have wondered why he did not take advantage of the Mahommedan law which allows several wives. I think he was right not to choose that solution. In the twentieth century it is no longer acceptable. It can only increase the number of complications and was justifiable only in the days when a woman had no existence outside the protection of a man and was incapable of ensuring her own livelihood. When the Prophet permitted the taking of four wives—and even, under certain conditions, extra concubines—there was an humanitarian reason behind it which no longer exists today. In Arab countries, before Islam, only boys were considered of importance and some of the girls were occasionally buried at birth. As for me, I do not think I would have agreed to be a second wife.

Fortunately, the question never arose. After his divorce, families naturally began to present a number of girls to the King and, from time to time, their photographs appeared in the papers. Then, at the School of Architecture—I was still in France at the time—my companions in the studio would ask me in fun: 'And why not you? You are very sweet . . .' And I used to answer in similar vein: 'But yes, why not me? Write to the King, perhaps he will listen to you.' We amused ourselves talking nonsense on the subject and I announced: 'If the King marries me, I shall invite you to Iran and we shall do this and that and you shall go with me to Shiraz and Ispahan . . .' and they carried it further with a sally about the homonymy between 'Shah' and 'chat' (cat). One of my girl friends though I would make a good queen and in the gardens of Aranjuez, during our Spanish journey, wrote on the back of a postcard: 'Farah Diba = Farah Pahlavi'. I have kept it.

But to me, it was never more than a happy jest. I was a girl like most others, still with something of childhood in my round cheeks and the curls across my forehead. I was just beginning to emphasise my eyes with a shy pencil, to put a little colour on my lips—in Iran, I would never have dared. I was barely interested in politics but I did sometimes meet argumentative young men who were only too ready to spread such propaganda as: 'We cannot return to Iran. There will be no work. All the good jobs are reserved for influential families.' I also had a girl friend with communist leanings who fulminated against the feudal structure of Iran and the absence of reforms. Student magazines were put into our pigeon-holes vilifying the King. I did not read them. I was very royalist, attached to the King and unquestioning. I do not recall ever criticising him, except once, when he was staying in Paris. When one is young, heads of state seen super-human, we feel they have no right to behave as we do, to go to the theatre or a restaurant. And I wrote to my mother: 'Why does the King stay in Paris? He ought to be in Iran.'

Life back there was indeed very difficult just then and the condition of the peasants almost wretched. I had realised that when I was very young, during my holidays in the provinces. Once, while staying in the country, I refused for three days to speak to one of my uncles, so angry was I that he had taken everything from a peasant caught stealing some corn. So I was not very well-informed about politics, but did nonetheless have a sense of justice and equality. I did not want some to have a great deal of money and others none, I was outraged by certain privileges that were an abuse. In my simplicity, I thought then that two or three new laws, a few extra schools and hospitals would put everything to rights. I had no idea that I was soon to face the reality of these problems and share the responsibility of solving them.

2

Do not find fault with me for the love that is mine

Do not find fault with me for the love that is mine;
If, in the school of life,
There had been taught some better art,
I would have learned it.

A PERSIAN POEM

I met the King for the first time at our Embassy in Paris. The Ambassador had chosen certain students who were doing well in their studies to present to him. He sent us an invitation, telling us we were to have the honour of being presented to the sovereign. It was very exciting. I wore what seemed to me both most appropriate and most becoming: a tight skirt of white, black and grey tweed, and a top with a buttoned-up collar and long full sleeves, to the front of which I had pinned a white camellia. I remember that because of a photograph which the journalists found later in their files: my hair was gathered back into a chignon and my fringe was thick and curled.

The King was in a corner of the big reception room at the Embassy and we passed before him one by one. I expect I made a little curtsey.

'What are you studying?' he asked me.

'Architecture, Majesty.'

'Do you not think that rather unusual for a woman?'

I must have stammered that I did. I believe he asked me if I had any difficulty with the French language and I told him that I had learned it in Teheran. That was all.

His voice was serious, calm and deliberate and I thought his eyes looked sad. But I was proud and happy because the Ambassador, in presenting me, had spoken very highly of me and the results I was achieving in my studies.

Afterwards, the students pressed closely around to talk to him. I remained at a slight distance, embarrassed by this lack of discretion. It seemed to me presumptuous and too familiar to hem the King in so closely, jostling one another only a foot or so from his person.

This meeting naturally made a great impression on me but the King has admitted to me since that he has no recollection of it, which is only natural. The following summer, it was in 1959, it so happened that I was able to return to Iran for the holidays. Like all the students at my School, I had to spend part of my time preparing an architectural study. I had chosen a mosque in Ispahan and drew plans, sketched the details of the mosaics, went to the museum to do research in old books and led a quiet life among my family and my girl-friends.

My father's brother, Esfandiar Diba, was at that time Adjutant to the King. So that I could discuss the possibility of a schlolarship, he introduced me to Mr Zahedi, who looked after Iranian students abroad. Mr Zahedi was the husband of the Princess Shahnaz, the King's only daughter by his first wife, the Princess Fawzia. He wanted to present me to the Princess and I was invited to her house. The King also came that day. Many girls of good family were being presented to him at that time and perhaps Princess Shahnaz and Mr Zahedi had some purpose in mind . . . But I was no fool and when I saw the King arriving, realised I was there to see if I pleased him or not. Fortunately, I was able—he has since told me—to continue behaving quite naturally towards him.

The King asked me questions and was very kind. I myself was very glad to meet him, to discover that I was talking to an ordinary mortal for, when one is young, one imagines that kings and queens live differently, walk differently, have their being somewhere beyond the reach of ordinary mortals. But the King is very approachable and very human. I spoke to him about studying in France and he told me very simply of his meetings with the students. I remember even having a slight difference of opinion with him. I made no attempt to play the courtier and agree with everything he said. If I thought differently, I said so.

Yet afterwards, every time I was to meet him, my heart beat fast at the thought of seeing him. I was very, very excited but as soon as I found myself once more in his presence, I became quite calm and natural again. I never tried to appear different, more intelligent, more elegant or more interesting. I remained as I always was. I did not want to behave as if he had already married me, as if it were already decided. I remained myself, pleasant and unaffected. It is an attitude that has always helped me in life.

We met a number of times afterwards at the house of the Princess Shahnaz. The King invited me to luncheon with him at the Palace, he took me up in his aeroplane and flew me over a part of Iran. Curiously, my memories of that month of September are very vague and confused. What was happening to me was so utterly incredible that I seemed to be living in a dream. There came a day when we were both sitting on a small sofa and the Princess and her husband apparently casually left the room, followed by the other guests. We were left alone. Very gently, the King told me he had already been married twice and that, as I knew, he had had to separate from these wives for reasons of State. He asked me if I would be willing to marry him. He added that I would, of course, eventually have heavy responsibilities, that I would have to be not only his wife but also serve our country at his side. I was deeply moved though, in my secret heart, I had thought it might happen. I do not know exactly how I replied, but I did accept.

He has told me since that he made up his mind at our first meeting at the Princess Shahnaz' house. It is, nonetheless, strange how things happen. I have said that when I was young, I dreamed of a husband who would be tall, fair and green-eyed. As for the King, he liked tall women—I did answer to that description—but preferred them fair-haired and fair-skinned, which I certainly was not.

'But what made you choose me in particular?' I asked him one day. 'What was it that struck you?'

'Your ease of manner and your unaffectedness.'

'But how were they apparent?'

'On the terrace at Shahnaz' house, we were playing quoits. They were going all over the place and you, without any fuss, bent down to pick them up. I liked that, for it meant you were without affectation.'

Then, I am sure that my appearance must also have pleased him. I was not beautiful, but he liked women to be tall. The King must have thought that, with me, he would perhaps have tall children. But when I look at photographs of that time, I am rather astonished at having attracted him: my cheeks were so round, my hair so dark and with those huge chignons, those incredible edifices which were then the fashion—the higher, the better.

As a woman matures, she learns to dress, to wear make-up and, although she no longer has the same freshness that she had at twenty, she acquires personality. It is perhaps odd, but frankly I prefer myself as I am today rather than as I was then. Sometimes, I jokingly say to my husband: 'You have a seeing eye. You knew that my looks, like a Kerman rug, would improve with time . . .'

I was in a state of euphoria, not fully aware of what was happening to me. I could not guess what lay ahead of me so I asked myself many questions. I was going to marry a King, but like any other girl about to wed, my first preoccupation was with the prospect of sharing my life with another. I felt considerable affection and love for him and since there had never been any other ties of affection before my marriage, it was very important to me. My mother, too, although proud, was rather anxious. She was not carried away at the prospect. What concerned her most was the happiness of her daughter. She wondered what my father would have thought of it.

But I was already seeing beyond my personal life and thinking of the responsibilities which would fall upon me as the King's wife. It was not just an ordinary marriage, I knew I would have to serve my country, to try to the best of my ability to find solutions to some of its problems.

Was I ready to become Empress? I do not know how one can learn this rarest of professions but my upbringing had taught me good manners and a sense of responsibility. I had been a cub mistress and captain of a basket-ball team and from these activities had learned a sporting spirit and to work as part of a team. I had lived quite alone in Paris and, having had to create a personal discipline for myself, realised both the importance and the limits of freedom. I had acquired a taste for making decisions and choices. Every experience in life, if it is properly understood, can be put to use in later years. During my engagement, I used to hear people saying, as they watched to see how I would bear myself: 'She might always have been a Queen.'

Without a doubt this impression arose from my certainty that I loved the King deeply. Among the many letters I received, most of them delightful, were others which asked rather maliciously: 'Why are you marrying him? He is old enough to be your father . . .' Those writers did not know that when two people love one another, each is the whole world to the other. And whatever the difference in age, I sometimes feel like a mother towards him, sometimes like his child or his sister—though I remain always, and above all, his wife.

After asking me to marry him, the King presented me to his family. Few people were there, only the immediate family. The Queen Mother was seated on a sofa in her drawing-room and I sat on a pouffe at her feet. Someone commented: 'She has sat on the pouffe!' But where did they expect me to sit? I could not, at my very first meeting with her, sit beside the Queen Mother, as that would indeed have been lacking in humility. I had heard it said that she was very authoritative, with a strong personality and that there had been certain differences between her

43

and Soraya. But with me, it all went very well. From the very beginning, she spoke frankly to me and I feel a great affection for her.

The Queen Mother is very interesting because she hides nothing of her personality. She speaks her mind to everyone, which is a likeable trait. I had also heard a great deal of the Princess Ashraf, the King's twin sister. I realised at once that she was very intelligent and unusual. She is also very active and very devoted to her country. The Princess Ashraf has always been kind to me, showering me with gifts and letters whenever she travels. The Princess Shams and the Princess Fatemeh, the King's other sisters, have also been very welcoming and very charming from the beginning.

I was calm, but certainly felt rather shy and it was only to be expected that they should be more at their ease than I. With great kindness, they asked me questions about my life, my family, my studies, my tastes and I replied as simply and openly as possible. But here again, I can remember none of the details. It felt like a dream and I allowed myself to be carried along by events. In any case, I felt no strain, for all that mattered to me was the opinion of the King. He had asked for me in marriage and in that lay my strength. He loved me and that was all that mattered. So I felt at ease with everyone else, the more so as I knew I had the friendship of the Princess Shahnaz who had presented me to the King, her father. I was glad to have known him through her.

It might be imagined that the person who presents you to a King would ever afterwards seek to dominate you to a certain extent. Princess Shahnaz never did. All she asked in exchange was our affection. She had been separated very young from her mother, King Farouk's sister, and perhaps had suffered from a certain loneliness during her childhood.

The Pahlavi enjoy a particularly close family life. We have always dined several times a week with one member of the family or another. This closeness is very dear to me and, each time we meet, my pleasure is renewed. I have never had any difficulties with my husband's family, except perhaps in that I have to be careful to share my affection equally. I am always very careful not to miss any family gathering, for fear of drawing upon myself such comments as: 'But what is the matter? Why did you not come? You do not love us any more!' Even after seventeen years of public life, I never have the right to feel tired or to have a headache. I am always afraid that, if I do not smile, people who love me may be hurt. I have suffered too much from the quarrels within my own family not to make every effort, even if it is sometimes rather difficult, to preserve harmony in my husband's circle.

It is the same in public life. I must never forget that I am always being watched. If I go to an inauguration, or to Parliament, people occasionally say to me: 'What has happened? Aren't you well, you did not seem to be on form? Were you annoyed about something?' And reply: 'What do you expect on such a solemn occasion? I could scarcely laugh!'

Before the official engagement, I had to go to Paris to buy my wardrobe, my wedding dress and to prepare my trousseau. Everyone wanted to accompany me, some to help me choose gowns, some to help me choose hats. In a way, it was rather embarrassing because I knew that all these ladies were very close to the Princess Soraya. From a human angle, it seemed to me rather disloyal to transfer allegiance in such a way. But, after all, their first allegiance was to the King so it was only natural for them to conform to his wishes. One word more: I have always admired those who have not tried to hide their attachment to the King's former wife in order to win my favour.

Everyone stared at me, looked at me as if I were some curiosity, watched with avid interest how I walked, sat or spoke. Similarly, and inevitably, compliments were showered upon me. It was natural that each should try to win my favour but I treated everyone alike.

I set out for Paris, therefore, with an uncle and two of my aunts. We stayed at the Hôtel Crillon. Every morning, we visited the boutiques and the shops. I had been given a free hand, expense was of no importance. The Rue Saint-Honoré, the Rue Royale, Dior, Carita and so on. In the mirrors of the great fashion houses I thought I looked terribly thin. The fashions were quite different from those of today and I dress now in a far more youthful style than I did then.

No one had been told officially that I was to marry the King but, by the time the plane landed at Geneva, the journalists knew. The airport was crammed with photographers. In my innocence, I thought there must be some minister travelling in the same plane as us. Then I saw them all running in every direction looking for the future Queen. This first experience of the press left me literally stupefied. In Paris, they followed me everywhere, ready to photograph every gesture, so desperately eager, with all their cars, that they created traffic jams on the Champs-Elysées. They would drive through all the red lights rather than lose me. At the Hôtel, no one ever said where I was going but there were journalists at every door. One of them even paid a Maître d'Hôtel to allow him to take his place on the floor where I was staying.

It was an incredible game of hide-and-seek. The photographers jumped on to the car to take shots and I was afraid they would be run over. The result was a whole series of photographs showing me with my mouth wide open in fear, a series used later by certain papers to prove that I was unhappy. The circus began at Orly, where there were so many flashlights that I was blinded and had to be taken by the arm and dragged along. I even lost my shoes. But it all remained good-humoured. I had studied in Paris, I spoke the language well, therefore I was good copy.

In any case, the French have always been kind to me, as if I belonged a little to their country, as if it was one of their daughters whom the King had chosen. I saw my friends there but, at the King's request, spoke to no one of my future marriage. I told only a few very close girl-friends and asked them not to tell anyone else.

To one of them:

'It seems that I am to marry . . .'

'Who?'

'Guess'.

'So-and-so? . . . So-and-So? . . . So-and-So?'

'No.'

'Then, that only leaves the King . . .'

'Yes, him!'

The others learned of it in the newspapers. After my return on 3 November, 1959, there was the official betrothal. A very small ceremony: members of the family on both sides, a few Ministers, the Presidents of the Chambers, certain members of the Court. I wore a sea-green dress, heavily embroidered but very simple, and no jewels. My hair was parted in the middle and gathered into a chignon in the style which became known for a time as the 'Farah Diba' style. Curiously, many people abroad still call me Farah Diba, as if it were a double first name. It was all very simple: the King gave me a ring and then there was tea and cakes. My youngest sister-in-law, Fatemeh, was to be married on the same day so, immediately after our betrothal, we went to the Queen Mother's Palace to be present.

In fact, it was in this house, which the Queen Mother lent me, that I spent the month before our marriage. I lunched every day with the King and we dined with members of his family. In those days the King had more spare time than he has today and we used to go for long drives, or riding and sometimes he would take me up in his plane. When I was young, I feared nothing. It was a very small plane which tossed considerably whenever there was any wind. One day, the undercarriage would not come down. Below, on the airfield, I could see numbers of ambulances and fire-engines. We were alone together in the plane and the King asked me to take a crank handle to try to dislodge the wheels. Fortunately, it all ended well. But when I fly today, immediately anything begins to vibrate, even slightly, I grow anxious. It is the same in a car. The King has always liked to drive fast. He used to drive at seventy-five miles an hour and I was not in the least afraid. But now, if he does more than fifty, I begin to tremble. Perhaps it is a question of age?

On our engagement, the western press had a headline: 'The Shah of Iran marries a shepherdess', or else they compared me with Cinderella, which shows that journalists know very little about their own fairy stories. They forgot that Cinderella, too, was the daughter of a King. I was, of course, just an ordinary girl, but of good family. These rather exaggerated comparisons irritated my family: 'You are not a nobody, you were not born a beggar. You come of an old family, an important family . . .' They were not very pleased to read in the papers that I was a so-called 'soldier's daughter' or other tales of the kind. But I could not make myself ridiculous by contradicting them: 'You are mistaken, I am not as you think . . .', the more so since, personally, it worried me not at all. Quite the contrary. This comparison with the people was in my favour . . . I was, indeed, a daughter of the people, since there is nothing in Iran which corresponds to western aristocracies, where titles of all kinds abound—prince, princess, marchioness, duke, baron and so forth. It is, of course, very fine to be able to claim noble descent, but the important thing is to be oneself.

The day of the marriage—21 December 1959—came at last. The previous day, I had tried on my dress, a Dior gown embroidered all over with paste jewels and pearls and edged with white mink, the veil, the mantle with its long train fastening with a wide bow in front and intended for the religious ceremony when my shoulders had to be covered. The Carita sisters had come to dress my hair, arrange the veil and the diadem. Their agitation was greater than anyone else's for, to them, it was a work of art. I put on the necklace and Crown jewels, the diamond coronet with the enormous rose diamond in front, the earrings and the diamond and emerald clasp. Incredible! I was carried along, passed from hand to hand and my real self continued to float on its own little cloud.

The next day, the Princess Shahnaz and the Court Chamberlain came to fetch me fom my uncle's house,

In Washington. *Above* with President and Mrs Ford, 1975.
Below with President and Mrs Carter, 1977

The Coronation; 27 October 1967. *Above:* The first Queen to
be crowned in the 2500 years of Persian dynastic history
Below: Walking in procession in the courtyard of Golestan
Palace after the ceremony

An official photograph

Above receiving the Chinese Vice-Premier Li Hsien-nien and his
wife in Teheran
Below with Chou En-lai, Peking, 1972

Above an unexpected meeting with King Hussein and the late
Queen Alia at Heathrow Airport, 1976
Below with President and Mrs Sadat, Cairo

An informal visit to Britain, 1976. With *above* the Queen Mother and *below* James Callaghan

where I had returned, to accompany me to the Palace where the ceremony was to take place. My mother, my aunt and a friend helped me to gather my train into the car. People cheered and waved. I replied, but not for one moment did it occur to me that, to them, I was just someone new replacing another they had known and that I might have to work to win their affection. I thought there already existed a sense of sympathy between us and that they loved me as much as I loved them.

In the Marble Palace, the little ten or twelve-year-old bridesmaids were waiting to carry my train. Before me, walked a small boy scattering white flowers in my path. At the entrance to the Palace, I passed beneath the Koran, as I had done on leaving my own home. Then I walked below the Islamic vaults of the immense Throne Room, lined with mirrors. On the floor, before the bride and groom, was spread a white cloth with another mirror to symbolise happiness, chandeliers to symbolise light, a piece of sugar to symbolise the sweetness of life, pieces of gold to symbolise the viaticum the girl would receive if the couple should separate, incense, the Koran, a goblet of clear water and some cakes. The Mohammedan priest recited verses from the Koran.

All my thoughts were on what we were doing and I was deeply moved. In Iran, custom requires the priest to ask the fiancée three times if she is willing to wed. One is not expected to reply immediately, but to wait until the third time of asking but, in my excitement, I said 'Yes' the first time I was asked. But, most amusing of all, was when the rings were exchanged and there was not one for the King. It had not for a minute occurred to me that it was I who had to buy it. So we had to temporarily borrow that of the King's son-in-law. Then, for the first time, I signed myself 'Farah Pahlavi'. It was not a very well written signature—I had not practised it—and I have had to go on writing it in the same way ever since. I was so bewildered that I cannot remember if anyone performed for me the Iranian rite of taking a needle and thread and making a few stitches to signify the silencing of one's mother-in-law's tongue!

Then, I opened a cage and set doves free as a token of happiness and peace.

For our wedding journey, we went to the shores of the Caspian Sea. Looking back on it now, at our little house there, it really was all very modest. Scarcely a house, rather a room built of wood and standing on piles in the harbour, very ugly and planned entirely as a departure point for water ski-ing. There were some rather rickety iron bedsteads and an assortment of old pieces of furniture. It was very, very spartan. But then, comfort was not in the least important—we enjoyed ourselves thoroughly and it was very much to our liking.

On our return, the King chose a Principal Private Secretary for me, then there were the first audiences, the replies to the letters of good wishes and congratulations. Little by little, my activities as a sovereign began.

At first, I was not very busy and had a great deal of free time. Often, I was at a loose end and sometimes felt rather bored. I did not foresee then that, today, I would want to do so many things and not have time for them. We went out every evening. Like most women, I had my own ideas on how a husband should show his affection and I used to think: 'My husband should be like this, or like that; he does not do this, or that . . .' 'Perhaps it is because of his position,' my mother explained. 'You must not behave like a spoiled child.'

In those days, communication between mothers and daughters was not very explicit. Today, mothers are ready to explain the natural things of life candidly to their children from a very young age. In my day, sexual problems were taboo, they were not mentioned. I never spoke of them to my mother. She was of a generation which considered it unseemly. With my own children, it is the opposite. If they ask, at the age of three, how they were born, I try to explain it to them. They are not to be satisfied with stories that they were brought by the stork and found in a cabbage or a rose. I had to learn entirely from personal experience that married life is a sharing, that each partner has to give a little of himself, to forget self and try to understand the needs of the other. That is why I insist so much on courses in the secondary schools and universities to prepare the young for marriage, so that they do not rush ignorantly into married life, only to divorce at the slightest difficulty.

In a marriage there are small details which do not appear important, but which are so. For example, the King is very punctual, while I am sometimes late. I tell myself that a quarter of an hour more or less is unimportant. Then he grows impatient and if we allow ourselves to become involved in an argument, we both arrive at our engagement in a state of irritation—which is a pity, even if it lasts no more than five or six minutes. Instead of replying: 'No, I am not late' or 'I don't mind being late', one should try to restore a husband's calm, to ask him if he likes your dress or if he would be kind enough to go and choose a piece of jewellery for you to wear. Obviously, these are only very minor incidents, but if they accumulate, they risk appearing more serious than they are. Conjugal harmony has to be learned.

Before my marriage, I had not thought for one moment about the question of children, yet this is of absolutely fundamental importance to the monarchy. I was solely preoccupied with the marriage itself. Only afterwards, when I felt everyone about me watching for the first signs of pregnancy, did it faintly occur to me that I might not be able to have a child or might have only daughters. I should have liked it to happen straightaway, and so, at the end of the first month, when I knew that I was not yet pregnant, I was very sad. I believe I even wept.

My sister-in-law suggested a visit to a doctor who would be able to help me increase my chances of bearing a son. So, two months after the wedding, this professor came to examine me, but he had no need to prescribe anything, for he quickly realised that I was already pregnant. I was delighted and there began then a period of very great happiness, of great tenderness between my husband and myself.

Immediately, there was talk of bringing famous gynaecologists from abroad, but I refused for I felt that the birth of a child is one of the most natural things in life, that we had sufficiently good doctors in Iran and that if I were to give birth to an heir, it would be only seemly for me to be attended by an Iranian. But for the birth of a first child, precautions must be taken and we thought it would be better for me to have the baby in a hospital rather than at home. But I did not want to go into a fashionable clinic and chose instead an ordinary maternity hospital in the south of Teheran which is free for poor families. It was my way of showing my love for our people.

One day, very early in the morning, the King drove me there. It was impossible then to preserve an atmosphere of order and calm. Everyone wanted to be there: the Queen Mother, my mother, my sisters-in-law, the Ministers. All were in a state of indescribable excitement. The women would have all liked to have been present in the operating theatre to be able to say afterwards—if it was a boy—that they had had the good fortune to be there at the birth of the Crown Prince, and perhaps to have the chance of announcing the news to the King.

On 31 October, 1960, our first son was born. The news was received with an outburst of joy, as the future of the dynasty was assured. He was to be named Reza, like his grandfather. In the rejoicings, I think I was almost forgotten and only my mother thought to ask: 'And my daughter, how is she?' I had been given rather too much anaesthetic and the doctor was becoming worried because I was taking a little longer than I should have done to recover consciousness. Then, gradually, I became aware of the nurse tapping my cheek and calling 'Majesty, Majesty . . .' Little by little, consciousness returned. My husband was there, holding my hand.

'Do you want to know what it is?'

'Yes,' I murmured.

'It's a boy!'

I burst into tears. 'My God,' I thought to myself, 'if I had had a daughter, what would have happened! Everyone would have been so terribly disappointed!'

The whole country was expecting a boy. Foreign journalists had come weeks before and taken up positions near the hospital to proclaim the news. From every part of the world, women had sent me lucky charms: a piece of lace from a cradle that had rocked only sons, an amulet with so-called magic properties . . . I had received, especially from France, piles of little blue shoes. People had written to tell me: 'Do not worry, I have read your fortune in the cards and it will be a boy.' To tell the truth, during my pregnancy I was not in the least concerned about whether it would be a boy or a girl. To me, it was my child. But after its birth, seeing the general rejoicing, I was happy to have fulfilled their hopes. And even as far away as France, a magazine bore, in Persian, the headline: 'It's a boy!'

The King wanted to go at once to a mosque to give thanks but he could not set foot outside the hospital so tightly packed was the crowd, acclaiming him, almost lifting his car from the ground. I knew from the radio that, for several days, there was spontaneous dancing every evening in the streets. Taxi drivers said: 'It is a day of rejoicing, there is nothing to pay.' Workers bought sweets or cakes to hand around. In the shops, the traders gave away their fruit to all the passers-by.

It was wonderfully comforting after the campaign of calumnies we had had to endure. One radio station called 'Free Iran', which broadcast from outside the country, had been spreading slanderous information. It claimed it was the King who could not beget children, that it was not true that I was expecting a child and that I was disguising myself in order to appear pregnant. And I, who was not then at my most elegant, was obliged to have myself photographed in order to reassure people and enable them to know the truth. All was grist to the slanderers' mill. This radio invented incredible stories, for example that I had gone to that particular hospital to take another child, and then, when my son was born, that the King was not his father. My child Reza, himself gave them the lie: he is the image of the King.

My husband granted an amnesty to a large number of prisoners. I stayed another week in the hospital, happy and with only one care: to spare my child as much as possible from the reporters' flashlights so that his sight might not be damaged. When I came out, I found flowers strewn all along my way. I sat in the car beside the King, with the baby in my arms. The demonstrations of affection all along our route brought tears to my eyes.

On 12 March, 1963, Farahnaz was born. What a joy that our second child should be a girl. This time, the baby was born in the Palace. In their excitement, the Princesses Ashraf and Shahnaz cried out so loudly that a poor Court official who had come to bring a Koran, slipped and fell down the stairs. In Persian, 'farah' means 'joy' and 'naz' means a caress. My daughter is very devoted to her father and when she was two or three years old, she always clung to him and would never let anyone else hold her when he was there. Like all fathers, the King was very proud of this and deeply touched. I afterwards gave birth, on 28 April, 1966, to Ali Reza, who is named after the King's brother killed in an aeroplane accident. I felt almost too fortunate to have exactly the children I wanted: a boy, a girl, then another boy but—to crown my happiness—my hopes were once again fulfilled when, on 27 March, 1970, Heaven sent us another daughter, whom we named Leïla.

I am very fond of children and would have liked to have more but since I was preaching family planning and asking others to limit the number of their children, I could not myself set a bad example. Besides, I feel that four is an excellent number, especially as it is already impossible for me to devote to them as much time as I would wish.

My husband and I wanted our children to have as normal an education as possible, feeling that considerations of protocol should take second place to ensuring that they enjoyed their childhood. They needed surroundings in which they could grow and develop. We did not wish them to be educated by private tutors so we founded a little bi-lingual school (French and Persian) in the grounds of the Palace with about sixty pupils from all social backgrounds, chosen solely for their aptitude for work. In this school, our children lead the lives of all school children of their age.

However, we could not ignore the responsibilities which the Crown Prince would later have to shoulder. He was already, at the age of three or four, taking part in official ceremonies at which he had to behave properly, which is not always easy at that age. The younger children have, of course, been less constrained. We explained gradually to Reza that he would later have important duties, but we told him only a little at a time so that his childhood should not be burdened or made fearful by the weight of responsibility he would one day have to bear. His apprenticeship to his future role as King has been gentle, by small stages, his activities increasing naturally year by year. At the same time, he was to be treated in school exactly like his young companions. He and his friends had to realise that there were times when they could call him Reza, play with him, do things just like all other children and other times—during offical ceremonies—when the relationship was different, when a certain distance had to be observed.

We have, above all, tried to teach Reza through the example of our own work and by talking to him about events as they happen. On a journey, whenever we stopped in some village, I would tell him of the local problems. He would be interested and consider, in his childish way, what he would do, if he were responsible for the village, to improve its standard of living in the space of two or three years. He would choose young people, send them to school so that one would become an engineer, another a doctor, yet another an expert in agricultural matters . . .

Sometimes, we would send our children incognito to the south of Teheran or to poor regions. When Reza discovered the poverty, the difficult living conditions of some families, he would grow very angry. 'Surely,' he would say, 'my father does not know it is like that, that there are such very poor people living in such very bad houses!' On his return, he would tell us what he thought and ask 'Why does not the Mayor try to do this or that?'

Then was the moment to explain to Reza that it takes time and that it is not possible to change everything all at once. We would take advantage of such moments to talk to him about the problems of the country, to tell him that material help alone does not solve every difficulty, that the important thing is to educate people and give them work. In this way, without going into too great detail, we gradually made him aware of matters of state. Reza is now more than sixteen and will shortly enter the Military School, as his father did. In his case, what matters is not that he should specialise in any one field but that he should acquire a thorough knowledge of his country and his people.

He will not, like the King, have to go abroad for some of his studies because, in the space of one generation, the education system of Iran has developed remarkably. This is an advantage. When his father was in Switzerland, he studied under a tutor so terrified of Reza Shah that he refused to allow him to ski, or swim, or even ride a bicycle. My son, on the contrary, has already piloted a plane. He can drive a car, he skiis, shoots, goes underwater diving and takes part in other activities which all help him to develop physically and which expand his creative spirit. He has, indeed, grown considerably recently and is now taller than his father.

Farahnaz, Ali Reza and Leïla, my three other children, are growing up happily together and are a daily source of great joy and deep satisfaction. But their education is, of course, less demanding. It has, however, to be accepted that they will never really be ordinary children and will probably always lack certain simple skills which can only be learned in the street or through material want, which they have not experienced, though they are aware of it from meeting people, from their travels and because it must be one of their constant preoccupations. I, myself, doubt whether, after so many years, I could cross a busy boulevard alone or shop for my family's meals.

And yet my own problems are not unlike those of all women who work and have children. I am very wrapped up in my work and feel it is a God-sent gift to have a great deal to do, even if I do sometimes regret not having more time to spend with my children. Dividing my time between my duties as a mother and my duties as Queen is often difficult, for there are thousands of other children throughout the country to whom I must also devote a part of my life. And, after all, is not the future of Iran, to which I am devoting myself, also the future of my own children?

I should not, however, wish it to be thought that the period of our life I have just described, in writing of my children, has always been entirely easy or free from difficulties.

I need only recall the endless intrigues of General Bakhtiar to overthrow the régime in the sixties, the riots and bloodshed in Teheran in 1963 or the assassination of the Prime Minister, Ali Mansour, in January 1965. I shall not describe these episodes which were often very difficult, sometimes terrible. Journalists and historians are better placed than I to do this. In any case, there is already an abundant literature about it all.

Nor shall I dwell long on the Revolution of the Shah and the People, for my husband has analysed it in depth in his own works and those who specialise in Iranian matters know it well. I shall only say that the twenty-sixth of January 1963, when it was promulgated, is without a doubt one of the most important dates in the history of modern Iran and marks a decisive turning point. The Social Charter which the King gave his country on that day signified a complete break with the feudal structures of the past. It put into effect a fundamental agrarian reform—in which the King himself gave the lead by distributing all his lands to the peasants— it nationalised all the natural resources, it offered workers a share in the profits of enterprises, it established universal suffrage and marked the beginning of an unprecedented effort in the fields of education and health. It benefited all, required the cooperation of everyone and immediately received tremendous popular support.

For me, it was a vital moment: these reforms, brought about through the efforts of the King, gave me faith in what I had undertaken and inspired the courage I needed to persevere in my task. If I had had to continue to work in a society in which there were so many economic and social injustices, my enthusiasm would have been far less. During a visit to Baluchestan, then one of the most backward provinces of Iran, I said spontaneously to the people who had come to see me: 'I, too, am a soldier of the Revolution.' I felt that was how it should be.

On 10 April, 1965, there was an incident which caused me very great distress. At about half past nine in the morning, the King arrived at the Marble Palace in town, where he worked. He was crossing the hall when, suddenly, a number of shots rang out. An ordinary soldier doing his military service in the Imperial Guard had made his way into the Palace, firing rounds from a machine-gun at everything in range. The two guards at the entrance panicked and fled. A servant tried to close the door, but in vain, and the killer advanced towards the King's office firing wildly. Two members of the Body Guard stepped in front of him with their little revolvers and the soldier immediately shot them. In his office, the King heard the shots but, not knowing what was going on, stayed where he was. A bullet penetrated the door, barely missing him. During this time, the exchange of shots had been fatal to the two brave members of the Body Guard who, before they died, had succeeded in killing the assassin. Suddenly, there was silence again, the King walked out and found the three corpses outside his door. It was a miracle that he escaped without a scratch. A few metres more and the crazed soldier would have penetrated his office . . . But, once order was restored, the King amazed his Private Secretary by resuming his daily work as if nothing had broken its routine . . .

I myself was unaware that anything had happened. I was getting ready for a meeting with the women of the Pahlavi Foundation when, suddenly, the telephone rang. At the other end of the line was the Queen Mother, in tears:

'Do you know what has happened?'

'No?'

'Someone has fired on the King!'

I gasped and my heart stopped beating. Terrified, I waited to learn more but the Queen Mother, between her sobs, could only repeat: 'Someone has fired on the King!' It took several seconds, which to me seemed centuries, before she managed at last to tell me what she should have told me first: 'Do not worry, all is well.' The shock had the most curious effect: I continued putting on my make-up, like an automaton, chanting: 'Thank you, God! Thank you, God!' Usually, my son, who was four and a half, accompanied his father. That day, his governess had taken him direct to the kindergarten to meet a small new boy. Otherwise, by slowing down his father's movements, he might have been with him in the path of the assassin's bullet . . .

Eventually, I saw the King, all was well and, immensely cheered by his calm, I was able to appear quite composed. Members of his family and friends arrived, pale with fear, and I spent some time reassuring and comforting them. My courage held for several days and then delayed shock set in. All the anxiety I had been holding in check came flooding back and I collapsed. The inquest revealed the ins and outs of the affair and they discovered that the wretched soldier had been brainwashed. The plotters and their confederates were arrested.

One night, some time afterwards, the King summoned one of the conspirators to the palace. I did not know about it but, chancing to come out of my bedroom—it must have been one o'clock in the morning—I saw this young boy, his hands bound behind his back, his face turned to the wall, before he entered my husband's study at the top of the staircase. I was filled with sadness and felt deeply sorry for him. My grudge was not against this man, but against all political systems, all subversive groups which manipulate the young and incite them even to murder. 'He is Iranian,' I told myself. 'With different people about him, he might have become a fine person, and this is what fate has made of him!' I was so sad that I wept at the thought.

The King talked to him for nearly an hour. Although he is without pity for those who attack the interest or security of the country, he always pardons those who attack only his life. The man was pardoned, as were his accomplices. One of them has an important position today in Iranian television.

Against all those who would like to exploit Iran or prevent it persevering with its reforms, the only obstacle is the King. Supporters of international terrorism used not to talk about it, but now they say openly: 'We want to kill the Shah because it is he alone who prevents us from spreading anarchy.' The risks of this situation have to be recognised and then put as much as possible out of mind. It is a part of our life. The King believes firmly in his destiny and in the will of God. He says: 'I shall be there as long as He thinks it necessary for me to be there.'

The King succeeded to the throne in 1941, but had never been solemnly crowned. He always said he did not wish to be consecrated King of a poverty-stricken people. But little by little, under his rule, reforms were put into effect which have changed the lives of the Iranians. The Charter of the Revolution of the Shah and the People brought greater justice and equality. Also, two sons had been born to him, the future of the monarchy was assured. So he thought the time had come to proceed with the coronation ceremony. It was decided that it should take place in 1967, on 26 October, his birthday, after more than a quarter of a century of difficulties surmounted and of effort to lead Iran along the path of progress.

It clearly had to be an occasion of solemn importance for the country. The ceremony could not, therefore, be improvised, but there was no ancient procedure to follow. We made a long search through the documents in the archives, looking especially for what could be best adapted to the special circumstances of our contemporary history. In particular, it was the first time for many centuries that an Empress was to be crowned. How should she be dressed? What crown should she wear? It was a great responsibility to decide these details for they would set a precedent. My crown was to resemble that of the Pahlavis, created by Reza Shah to resemble that of the Sassanids. We consulted numerous jewellers and many sketches and designs were submitted to us. In the end, Van Cleef and Arpels produced the best design, both the prettiest and the most suitable. M. Arpels came to Teheran and in the treasure deposited in the Melli Bank was able to find the stones he needed: emeralds and fine pearls set off with diamonds.

The gown I wore had to be different from those of western Queens but, on the other hand, no miniature provided any pattern of purely Iranian inspiration. That is why it was plain and in white. The important thing was to adapt the mantle and its train to our traditions. It was to be of green velvet, the colour of the descendants of the Prophet. Patterns were designed by Marc Bohan of Dior, according to our directions but the gown and the mantle were cut, assembled and embroidered in Teheran by Iranian dressmakers. Because of the length of the train, they had to work in the Officers' Club, where there were some very large tables.

My husband had no such problems. Everything was already in existence in the Pahlavi inheritance. The Crown Prince, who was seven, was to wear a smaller version of the same uniform and would be given the little sword which his father had worn at almost the same age at the coronation of Reza Shah, forty-one years before.

Then the ceremonial had to be laid down, the state arrangements made, the order of precedence determined. All the details had to be worked out. Who would hand the King his crown, who would pass him his belt, who the sceptre and other objects involved in the sacring? It had to be timed exactly to the minute, the King's speech had to end at midday, the hour at which, in all the mosques of Iran, from the top of the minaret, the muezzin calls the faithful to prayer. We had only one rehearsal, but thanks to it there were only very minor hitches on the great day: in order to put on the imperial belt, the King took off his uniform belt, but there was no one behind him to take it and it fell to the ground; my crown was not put on exactly right and some of my chignon escaped. The hairdresser was in a terrible state. But none of these mishaps was very serious.

Certain special improvements were to be made to the ancient Palace of Golestan for the occasion and that is what saved it, for in making them, the workers realized that it was on the point of collapse. Worm-eaten beams, rotten floorboards, cracked walls. Behind the portrait of Reza Shah was a crack an inch or two wide. It was in this Palace that we usually housed our foreign guests. Without the repairs that were made, the roof might have fallen on their heads! Stands were set up in the gardens and we prayed it would not rain. When the day came, the sky, thank God, was cloudless.

The Crown Prince entered the throne room surrounded by military and civil officers of the Household and followed by members of the Court. Then I entered with my ladies and the officers of my guard of honour in full-dress uniform. When everyone had taken their place, the King entered, to be greeted by magnificent choirs singing. During the moment of recollection, the Imam recited prayers and verses from the Koran. The King assumed the imperial insignia, the belt and golden sword encrusted with precious stones, the cashmere mantle embroidered with pearls. Then, with great solemnity, he took the scarlet crown of the Pahlavi, raised it above his head and, as his father had done before him, crowned himself. Who else was there to do so? He reasoned this way: 'I represent the people of Iran. Through my hands, it is they who crown me.' The sceptre of Reza Shah was handed to him. I went towards him and while the ladies-in-waiting placed the mantle on my shoulders, he crowned me in my turn. The King then took his seat on the Peacock Throne and, after his speech and those of the Prime Minister and the President of the Chambers, his brothers came to greet him in token of submission, congratulation and loyalty.

The ceremony, with its very beautiful singing, had been extremely impressive and moving throughout. My sisters-in-law, the Princess Shahnaz and I myself were all in tears as we saw the King crowned after so many years. It was fortunate that we had had that rehearsal for, in our emotion, we would otherwise certainly have made mistakes. For my son, it was also an event of the greatest importance and he bore himself splendidly. For his age, he maintained from the beginning to the end of that very solemn occasion, all the seriousness one could wish, despite the fact that he was the first to enter the Throne Room and the last to leave it. Yet he was slightly unwell and tired for he had caught a chill the day before. In fact, he won a great success, the Anglo-Saxon journalists saying he was the star of the show that day!

The muezzin's litany rose into the limpid sky above Teheran. We climbed into the carriages, the King and I in front, the Crown Prince, quite alone, behind us. When the horses moved off, I nearly lost my crown. Luckily no photographer was there, otherwise a picture of it would have graced all the sensation-mongering papers next day. Along our route, the pavements were packed with an ecstatic crowd, cheering at the tops of their voices and thunderous in their applause.

As I waved, I thought how truly the King deserved his crown: for having overcome so many great difficulties and for all that he had given of himself to his people and his country. I did not yet have the same claim on their gratitude but I felt that, through me, all the women of Iran had received the same diadem from the hands of the King who, in this way, gave them the place they deserved in our society. I was very proud, too, to be the first Empress of Iran to be crowned for so many centuries of its history.

3

What you must give

*If you exercise power, what you must
give is mercy; if you possess wealth, it is
generosity; if you have learning, you
must provide action and if you have the
gift of words, you must spread wisdom.*

IMAM ALI

When the King asked me to join my life to his, he warned
me that I would have to carry heavy responsibilities and
serve Iran at his side, but he did not explain that day
exactly what these duties would be. There were no
introductory sessions to initiate me into my tasks as
Queen.

Remember that I was only twenty-one years old and
my horizon was very limited. It took me, therefore, several years to really get to know my country, to begin to
take a more active part in some of the affairs of state, to
gain assurance in isolating problems and trying to find
solutions to them. From the very beginning, I naturally
and automatically became President of many organisations, I received all kinds of people to talk about the most
varied subjects, I went to inaugurations or paid offical
visits. But I used to wait until I was told what to do. I
thought that everything at Court happened in a pre-
scribed manner and that all I had to do was to conform
obediently. It did not enter my head that I could already
command: 'Do this, or that!'

Besides, when I sometimes said: 'It must be like this,' I

64

would be told: 'It has always been like that.' 'Oh well,' I would think privately, 'it has always been like that and therefore cannot be changed.' But gradually, through my daily work, through experience and contact with the representatives of the different organisations, and thanks to the help my husband always gave me when I needed him, I felt increasingly that I could take initiatives and launch myself usefully into action.

As time went by, the King gave me greater power and unloaded some of his own responsibilities on to me. Just before the coronation, he gave me very great proof of his trust by deciding that if, which God forbid, he should die before the Crown Prince reached his majority, it should be I who would assume the regency of the kingdom. A few years earlier, the King had summoned together the most senior of the civil and military officials to make known to them his political testament and to tell them what he expected of them should any mischance befall. But I am certain that, without him, nothing would be easy. On the world map, Iran is a country which cannot be ignored. If the King were no longer there to defend its interests, a number of foreign countries would probably try to take advantage of the situation in an attempt to extend their influence in our country. It was done once before, in the days of the Qadjar, when the monarch had to consult the ambassadors of England or Russia before making decisions.

The Pahlavi put an end to this dependence but there are those outside our borders who may not have forgotten it. Do you not imagine that they have plans filed away for subversion suited to any kind of political incident? But the interests of those who may look covetously upon Iran are so divergent that they will not combine to facilitate their task. If such a situation arose, who knows what ambitions for power might not be let loose within the country itself. This concern about potential dangers like these, led my husband to decide to settle the succession in advance. Anxious to keep the Crown Prince out of the grasp of factions, he considered that only his mother would be close enough to him to think solely of his good. The King also thought that I, who lived with him and shared his work, was the one best placed to understand his purpose and to carry it on. He knew, too, that the increased share of the people in his policies of independence and development would give me the support I would need, even if some retrogressive minds were still prejudiced against a woman exercising the supreme power. I hope, in any case, that in eighteen years, I have been able to prove my devotion and, if the worst should happen, I would devote myself entirely to trying to maintain the progress achieved by the Revolution of the Shah and the People. The King's basic aim is to lay a track along which Iran will be able to go forward with the minimum of help from himself.

But having said this, I pray God with all my strength never to have to live through such events. I find my present position just right: I have responsibilities, but not the very weighty, important ones of a sovereign; the areas with which I am concerned can bring only joy or satisfaction whereas a Head of State has sometimes to take decisions which arouse discontent. In the division of our task, it is I who have been given the better part.

However, this does not mean that I hold a sinecure. As the years have gone by, the scope of my activities has widened considerably. That is why my personal office consists today of more than a hundred and fifty people and I receive there nearly sixty thousand letters a year. The staff is now well acquainted with my manner of dealing with correspondence and hence only come to me for an opinion in special cases. It would be impossible for me to see everything. My Private Secretary brings me only a selection of the mail from Iran or abroad, the most significant of the personal cases, the reports of the various organisations over which I preside, messages from international organisations or offices with which we are connected, reports on current projects. I keep what seems to me to merit further thought, dictate my replies or comments on the remainder and tell him what I consider to be the priority of the moment.

My correspondents are as varied as the problems they

set before me: student scholarships, sick people who would like treatment abroad, unemployed people seeking work, young men hoping to be exempted from military service, quarrels between neighbours or relatives, complaints against local officials, private individuals who have problems with the administration or think they are victims of injustice—such, for example, as the university professor who bought himself a piece of land which the Ministry of Housing and Town Planning afterwards requisitioned in order to complete a building project, and who considers he has been insufficiently compensated; a retired professor points out ways in which, in his opinion, the educational system might be improved; requests for help or backing in securing a loan or a house. God knows how many people there are who need housing. I try to help them as best I can but I cannot offer each of them a house, it just is not possible.

There are also requests for transfers—the wife works for the government in one town while the husband has been sent to another. Many ask for money. This we normally refuse, in order to discourage begging and because there would otherwise be no end to it, but we never leave a letter unanswered. We try, rather, to find employment for the husband or the children. There are all kinds of letters, from the humblest, who ask for very little, to those who describe the most complicated situations. Some write to me only as a very last resort. Others have not even thought of first trying to solve their own problem. Some merely tell me the story of their life and ask me to find a solution.

We try to show them all that when there is a problem, we are there to serve the people. Obviously, it is impossible to solve everything but we must convince people that we consider what they say to be important and that those responsible do truly study with care everything that comes before them. Even what seems futile to us may be of basic importance to some family. Our duty is to try, as far as possible, to put ourselves in the place of others. But I hope that, in the future, if the administrative reforms are properly applied, most of the questions sent to us today will be settled at village or town or provincial level and will no longer all come to us. For, on account of distances, it sometimes takes us a long time to achieve a result. People do not always appreciate this. They present a letter and, two days later, ask me: 'Well, what has been done?' They want a reply straight away, as if their problem were the only one on our files.

There is an Imperial Inspectorate to which anyone may apply in case of difficulty. No matter who may be involved, this body will conduct a very thorough inquiry and, if it feels it necessary, refer the matter to the King. It is rather like what was known in the time of the Achaemenians, as 'the eyes and ears of the King'. It is composed of very honourable officials in whom the people have confidence and we rely on their reports. If I consider that certain matters need deeper investigation on the spot, it is to this organisation that I send the letters.

There are those who exaggerate and dramatise their case, but there are also people who, from modesty, do not explain in their letters the full extent of their cares. It is therefore often necessary to check, even though thousands of problems are submitted to us.

Each time I open a letter, I say to myself: 'Dear God, let it be a problem about which I can do something!' It is such a great joy to be able to give comfort and so distressing to be unable to help. I have a passionate wish to be of service and to bring help to every form of distress. Some problems are truly heart-breaking and it is impossible to remain indifferent to them. I feel a responsibility in the matter and use every possible means to try to find a solution. If I did not, I would never sleep peacefully.

Since I devote at least eight hours a day—and sometimes longer—to my work, it is obvious that there is more to do than to deal with mail. I am not content to preside in an honorary capacity over certain institutions, organisations, foundations or senior committees. I take an active part in them. We had to create a certain number of senior committees to coordinate the activities of the public and private sectors so that the budgets spent and

the staff engaged should be used to the best advantage
and for the benefit of the country as a whole, within the
framework of the development plans which had been
carefully worked out and were intended to be applied
throughout the land. For instance, it is necessary to
ensure that there should not be several clinics in one
town and none at all in a neighbouring one, that there
should not be two organisations working simultaneously on the same problem in the same region.

I am particularly interested in the senior committee on
town-planning. The problems with which it deals—the
quality of life and the environment in which the people
of Iran live—are today of great importance from a social
point of view. There is much building in Iran and if care is
not taken, we risk spoiling our historic patrimony, all the
monuments and ancient towns which are a part of the
spirit of our country. In conforming to the realities and
necessities of today, we must not lose sight of this cultural aspect. Until recently, there was no town planning
in Iran and it is one of our tasks to make people understand the need to plan such towns as, for example,
Ispahan, which is growing very fast but must not be
allowed to do so at the expense of the beauty for which it
is internationally famous.

All this is a part of the process of development of a
country like ours, and requires a great amount of time.
People in the provinces think that everything built in
Teheran is beautiful and that everything in their own
town is ugly. But we live in a country with widely differ-
ing climates which give rise to different styles of architecture and true beauty comes from building in a style
suited to the region and the local temperatures. Some, in
their anxiety to follow the example of the spreading
capital, are capable of building a modern house in the
desert where, from the very first, it will look ugly and, as
time goes by, prove ill-adapted. Skyscrapers of plate-
glass inevitably suffer from wind and heat. It is not for
nothing that the natives of the area spend much of the
summer in the basements of their low houses: it is fifteen
degrees cooler there than in the apartments of these

modern buildings in which people literally 'fry'. We try to respect both beauty and comfort.

There are also senior committees for research, social affairs, medical care, tourism and education. There is also the Research Institute for Agrarian and Peasant Affairs, very important in my view because a large proportion of our population lives in the villages and there is still a disparity between the standard of living in the towns and that in the country and it is as important for us as for other countries to study all agricultural systems in order to discover the best and the most suitable.

I could not write in detail of all the organisations over which I preside and in which I take a very active part, in the realms of education, health, culture and social matters. It would need a further book. A simple list will perhaps give some idea: the Organisation for Family Well-being—nurseries for the children of working mothers, teaching women and girls to read, professional training, family planning; the Organisation for Blood Transfusion; the Organisation for the Protection of Lepers; the Organisation for the Fight against Cancer; the Organisation for Help to the Needy; the Health Organisation, which works along the same lines as the World Health Organisation; the Children's Centre, the Centre for the Intellectual Development of Children—which I founded twelve years ago; the Imperial Institute of Philosophy; the Foundation for Iranian Culture; the Festival of Shiraz; the Teheran Cinema Festival; the Iranian Folk-lore Organisation; the Asiatic Institute; the Civilisations Discussion Centre; the Pahlavi University; the Academy of Sciences. . . . I shall describe only a few of them, either because they are closely connected with us or because they interest me particularly.

The Farah Pahlavi Foundation is a centre for orphans. Our original idea was simply to provide them with shelter and food. But before long, the Foundation was looking after thousands of children—nearly eight thousand now, throughout Iran—and we found ourselves faced with the problem of their education, which is very much more complicated than in the case of other children. We have continually tried to improve it, as well as the conditions in which they live so that the centres shall not remain comfortless, sad orphanages. In an effort to make the children's lives as normal as possible, we try to dress them better, to cut their hair in different styles, to preserve each child's individuality, to avoid putting them into dormitories of sixty at a time, to decorate their rooms, not to think of them as numbers. I have given much thought to every detail, preferring the names of flowers, instead of numbers, on their doors and their beds.

I consider everything concerned with very early childhood and motherhood to be of primary importance. The Organisation for Mothers and the New-born arose from this care. It is undertaking studies of the mothers and their diet, research into the new-born, it puts family planning into practice and owns big hospitals that are entirely free. The Organisation for the Protection of Childhood concerns itself with distributing vitaminised biscuits and milk to children living in areas where there is malnutrition. It also looks after handicapped children. For the latter, there are now special schools and this is a very great step forward because some people used to think: 'Why spend money on children like that? It is an unprofitable investment.' They were wrong, both on the human plane and economically, too, for many such children, if properly cared for, can become productive. Indirectly, that helps their families enormously for it removes some of the tension from their problem.

In the field of health, one of the most wonderful organisations is that which cares for lepers. A few years ago, leprosy was still a fairly widespread disease in Iran. It is one of the most terrible, in that those who are stricken with it have suffered for centuries not only from the physical malady but also from the fear they arouse in others. Fourteen years ago, when this organisation was founded, very few doctors or nurses were prepared to care for these people. Only a few members of Christian religious orders were willing to do so and the hospital conditions were terrible, just like those of the Middle

Ages. I always like to judge things for myself and I have seen the deep sadness of these people and the conditions in which they lived. I dreamed of it for nights. Each visit upset me for weeks. The only comparison I can find is a macabre one but, alas, it corresponds quite closely to the reality: a Fellini film, but without the characteristic humour. The first time I went to visit them, I took cakes for the children. Someone accompanying me took them and threw them at the patients. I shall never forget that scene: everyone around me was terrified at the idea of touching a leper.

My purpose in going to see these unfortunate people was to show that I intended to help them and to prove to others that one must not be so afraid of the disease, that it is not as contagious as popular tradition claims. So I insisted on approaching them. Some had but half a face, others had no hands or feet but, to set an example, I talked to them as if they were ordinary people, as naturally as possible, and I shook the hands of those who still had one. The women embraced me or touched my face as if I had the power of healing. Some, who had lost a lip, spattered my cheek with their saliva as they spoke to me but I acted as though nothing had happened.

The physical and moral distress of these outcasts was so poignant that I arranged for the Organisation for Help to Lepers to have any funds it needed. It is one of the most advanced research centres in the world into leprosy and its diagnosis. Unfortunately, leprosy is an insidious and tenacious disease which sometimes takes several years to show itself and there are still many lepers—about two thousand in our centres, nearly ten thousand known cases in the country and perhaps several thousands as yet undiagnosed. The King made a gift of land on which we have built a village for lepers who have been cured—cleansed, as they say. At first, the World Health Organisation was hostile to this idea. It did not realise the fear which lepers arouse in country districts, even when they are completely cured. But the result has been splendid. It is a village like any other, with houses and shops. The people live and work on a cooperative basis, cultivate acres of land and raise flocks of sheep. They are so very successful that the people of the region now come sometimes to visit them. We have not put the lepers back into society, it is society which has come to the lepers.

One of the most spectacular spurs to progress in the field of health began with a clause in the Charter of the Revolution which instituted the 'Army of Hygiene'. It is composed of young people, graduates of the Faculty of Medicine or others who have received an intensive course in that field and who, instead of doing their military service in the army, choose to work for two years in villages where there are no doctors. It is, indeed, very difficult for a young graduate in medicine to decide to practise in some remote place. Normally, a person in that position would hope to earn more money and have wider opportunities in a big city. That is why the King devised and created the 'bare-foot doctors' scheme. There is, of course, no question of these young boys and girls taking the place of real doctors, but at least in villages lost in the desert they are capable of teaching people the rudiments of hygiene, of treating minor ills —headaches, diarrhoeas or colds, for instance—of dealing with straightforward births in the best conditions possible and, in serious cases, of giving first aid before sending the sick to the nearest hospital or calling in someone more competent than themselves.

From a medical point of view, this experiment is a great blessing, for these pioneers, using very simple means, manage to reduce the mortality rate considerably and to carry elementary notions of hygiene into the most god-forsaken places. In the field of education, the situation is similar. Some villages are so small, so isolated, that it is practically impossible to set up schools and appoint permanent teachers, nor can people be asked to travel to distant towns for their education. So, following the same system, the King has created the 'Army of Knowledge' which makes no pretence to teach literature or applied mathematics, but which does teach reading, writing and counting to those peasants who are most cut off from knowledge. The young graduates who serve in this new army have made notable progress in reducing illiteracy in the country areas.

The problem of education is of prime importance, for it is the *sine qua non* of the progress which will admit us into the ranks of the developed nations. That is why I attach great importance to this aspect of my activities. Perhaps our most extraordinary contribution in this field is the Institute for the Cultural and Intellectual Development of Children and Young Adults. At its head is one of my two closest friends, who studied librarianship in America. The second of these two friends is in charge of the Farah Pahlavi Foundation. I am fortunate to have them both with me. Having known them all my life, I have complete trust in them and, furthermore, they really do give the best of themselves for, in addition to their responsibility to their country and to mankind, they also carry the heavy responsibility of their friendship for me. I greatly admire the achievements of this Institute and its utility to the country is proven. What is particularly wonderful is that what has been created rests upon no precedent and therefore everything can be new and vigorously pursued. Before its foundation, Iran had no library and very little literature for children. Only a few ancient tales. The Institute, therefore, really did start from nothing.

We began by collecting existing books and having translations made of foreign classics for children. I myself translated Hans Anderson's *Little Mermaid* and illustrated it in the style of Walt Disney. Symbolically, this book, with its accompanying record, was the first Iranian publication—by this organisation—to be entirely directed at very young readers. Afterwards, Iranian writers and painters had to be interested in this kind of literature, which until then had been unknown to them. We created this basic sector of education out of nothing. I am a very great believer in reading. Unfortunately, Iranians are not much given to reading because of the tradition of oral story-telling and the widespread illiteracy. Education had to be given an entirely new direction, and we had to try to accustom people to reading from a very early age.

In the beginning, not seeing too clearly where we were headed, the first members of the Institute simply took a case of books to a school in the south of the town to see what the reaction would be. The children threw stones at the car. But, little by little, they have grown used to it, have begun to take a great interest in their books and the Institute has made considerable progress. It has already built more than one hundred libraries in the towns, more than a thousand in the villages and has also created mobile libraries for the nomadic tribes. So books are reaching the children even in the depths of our deserts, sometimes, if need be, on the backs of donkeys, mules or even camels. We also have an extraordinary lorry which, within twenty minutes, can be transformed into a stage. It scours the countryside, presenting plays in places where people have never before seen a play or a film. Now, children take books home to read to their parents. They pass on what they learn at our centres to their families at home, from the most elementary matters such as how to comb hair or brush teeth. To a certain extent, the sons are educating their fathers.

Our concern with the fundamentals of education and its wider diffusion does not mean that we have neglected higher education. Indeed, the Institute of Philosophy, of which I am President, has set its aims very high indeed. Its researches start from the question: 'What has Persian civilisation given to the world? What can Iran still contribute?' The first question can be answered at once by stating that the world would certainly not be what it is without our contribution. Without going back to the controversial traditions which claim that our ancestors were the first to invent writing and to tame the horse, Persia gave birth to the great forerunners of medicine, mathematics and modern astronomy. Furthermore, some of our philosophers and great poets have influenced generations of western thinkers and writers. Malraux has said: 'The world owes much to the history of Persia' but under Graeco-Roman influence, many Europeans have forgotten it. In our own country, the memory of it is dimmed by wars and the blighted hopes of our own history. The first aim of our Institute of Philosophy is to give fresh life to our ancient works of art and our thousand-year-old culture so that they may be known to all.

And the future? Today, the world is seeking a new path, new systems and a new meaning to life. Industrial-isation, the material progress brought by the parallel roads of capitalism and socialism, no longer suffice. How to preserve human and spiritual values and at the same time encourage progress towards development? Here, perhaps, Iran has something to contribute. This search must indeed be one of the essential preoccupations of a country which, without any period of transition, has advanced in fifteen years from the Middle Ages to the last quarter of the twentieth century. Iran is a junction, for it is a country in which the very ancient traditions of history meet the entirely modern power which springs from the possession of very considerable natural resources. Its rate of development—one of the fastest in the world—permits it to devote itself to seeking that new path for which so many countries are hoping. The Char-ter of the Revolution of the Shah and the People is the foundation of a completely new political philosophy. The Institute has the task of determining its implications, developing its ideas and bringing them face to face with the realities of the contemporary world. I do not know if other nations will find in all this something to meet their aspirations. In any case, that is not our primary purpose. The essential is to advance towards progress in harmony with what I have called our 'Iranity'.

This wish to make our culture known and to enrich it by contact with others has brought me, through the Festival of Shiraz (the cherished and turbulent child of my love for art), the greatest joys—and perhaps also the greatest number of worries. The Festival is the meeting place of East and West. The most traditional and classical of plays are mingled with avant-garde works from all over the world. Today, it is world-famous and runs smoothly, on wheels as it were, but when we began it twelve years ago, it was a real adventure. We were all beginners, but brimming over with good will and the organisers took as much pains over it as if it had been their own idea. They worked night and day. The greatest in the land were ready, if necessary, to gather up the rubbish, to carry chairs, to hand round food and drink. There was an enthusiasm, a spirit of cooperation that will never again be equalled. Lodgings, transport, everything presented problems but we were able to call for help on anyone at all, from the Governor to the army. I remember telephoning my husband at about one o'clock in the morning because a double-bass player was stranded at Teheran airport, and asking if a military plane could land at Shiraz in order to bring him. On the first evening of an open air festival, there is always something that goes wrong. As the audience fell silent, we realised that the generator hummed very loudly indeed. While Rubinstein was playing, a cat walked across the stage. Or a sand storm would suddenly blow up and the orchestra's scores would fly away like swallows . . .

One had to be everywhere, to think of every single detail and then, when the show was over, there began the press conferences. Foreign journalists seemed to have come solely to act as self-constituted judges. Then, Iran and its problems had to be calmly explained to them. Sometimes, that went on until two o'clock in the morning. I always lost half a stone during the Festival. I wanted to see everything and have a share in all the programmes. Unfortunately, this became increasingly difficult because of problems of security. And then, each year the artistes asked for things that were increasingly extraordinary or entirely new. We would carefully organise for them some especially chosen place. They would not like it. They would go in search of some corner in the bazaar, to set up their stage in some shed. At first, we were bewildered, but in the end it made everything easier. We had been afraid of not having enough seats or sufficient equipment. Now we know that they are happy to use anything—all the old caravanserais, the most winding of streets, the pokiest of corners.

Bob Wilson's show lasted seven days and seven nights, up hill and down dale. He absolutely had to have an elephant, a snake and goodness knows what else beside! . . . As for Peter Brook, in his search for a new theatre, we had helped him create an international company which spoke onomatopaeically, without any precise meaning, inspired in part by the ancient Pahlavi tongue of the time of the Achaemenians and by Zoroastran songs. His show was given in two parts, one part in Persepolis and the other somewhere outside. So, once the first part was over, the company set off for the 'somewhere outside'. There, a soldier who had not been forewarned, told Peter Brook: 'You cannot go in' and refused to budge. Peter Brook naturally took umbrage. Half an hour later, I arrived in a jeep but in the middle of the road people were making signs at us. I stopped. Among them was one of the Directors of the Festival, livid and exasperated. I asked him: 'What is the matter?'

'Peter Brook is angry and refuses to continue his show.'

'That is not possible. Whatever is going on?'

'He is angry because the sentry refused to let him in.'

The poor Director, who had tried so hard, who had rushed here and there, climbed the mountain on foot to make sure that the lights Peter Brook wanted were properly prepared, was exhausted. He told me the actors had gone to supper in a small restaurant nearby. What was to be done?

The actors were angry. If I, too, lost my temper and went away, it would have been the end of everything. If I stayed and argued, the Iranians would not like it, and would feel insulted: no one keeps their Queen waiting for half an hour. So off I went to Peter Brook and told him: 'But these things happen. He is only a soldier, you know. You are quite right, someone from the Festival should have accompanied you to see that you were not stopped. But they did not and now it is too late to remedy it. You speak of kings and queens and you consider yourselves artistes. At this moment, it is I who am behaving like an artiste and you who are behaving like a king!' So, they set off towards the hills, in the neighbourhood of the tombs of our Achaemenian Kings, and then the play began. It was two o'clock in the morning, and it had all been planned to end with the rising of the sun. All these spectacles were extraordinary experiences.

Last year, the Rumanian, Andrei Serban, produced the Greek plays *Electra*, *Medea*, *The Trojan Women*. Even the memory of it stirs me still, for it was magnificent. For four or five hours, we stayed in Persepolis, walking behind the actors. They used the entire countryside and all the ruins, the hills and the columns, setting up scaffoldings here and there, speaking a language composed of a few Greek words but above all of cries, mingled with sounds, dances and music. People followed them like sleep-walkers, hypnotised. Through them, we became a part of the grandeur that is Persepolis. Followed by the spot lights, we were everywhere, the actors were in our midst, we were among the actors . . . It was quite unforgettable!

At the very beginning, in the first years of the Festival, people either laughed or were shocked. These extraordinary spectacles were so new to us. But little by little, understanding has come, people have grown accustomed to them and are intensely interested.

Xenakis, too, came to create something unique in the colonnades of Persepolis. It was *Persephasa*, with the audience in the centre surrounded by the orchestras. Forced, as he was, to stay well away from Greece, he was able here to indulge his love for stone carvings and he greatly enjoyed the Festival, defending it because he believed in it, even to the point of being criticised by his friends of the Left. Now he, too, is angry with Iran, but I hope it will not last.

Some of the entertainments were mad and rather daring: *Zartan* by Jerome Savary, for instance, which made the Iranians ask themselves: 'Should I go or should I stay away? What will people think if I go?'

Then the Bread and Puppet, a very interesting American group. They began by saying that, because of their imprisoned friends, they did not approve at all of the people organising the Festival. But they gave their entertainment nonetheless. Afterwards, they played in English under the walls of the prison in Shiraz. They tried to incite the people into action, and nothing was done to hinder them. They were not all like that.

Stockhausen played in the caravanserai of Shiraz and there was an extraordinary bond of sympathy between this modern music and the people in the bazaar who had never before heard anything like it. Everyone knew M. Stockhausen and the stall holders would greet him politely because he had given concerts for them in the streets. For devotees of classical music, contemporary music sounds strange. For those who have no musical knowledge, there is nothing to shock, so they are perhaps more receptive. I wonder if Stockhausen has ever had a more attentive audience than the simple, be-turbanned little workmen in the Shiraz bazaar?

All this takes place in an atmosphere that is infinitely appealing. People go from some very eccentric play to a highly traditional one and afterwards discuss them for hours: some are for Grotowski, others for Peter Brook, all are ready to cross swords in defence of their own conception of theatre . . . It is a completely relaxed setting, people dress as they like, usually carelessly, unconcerned with elegance.

At the first Festival, I wore a long gown and a tiara for the opening evening but, as the days went by, in keeping with the spirit of the occasion, my style of dress became increasingly informal until, in the end, I looked almost like a hippie.

The cultivation of knowledge is one of my foremost preoccupations. I consider that art is almost as necessary to man as bread. A few years ago, the organisations responsible for awarding scholarships were interested only in the technical professions useful to the immediate needs of the country: engineering, nursing, medicine. They hardly ever gave scholarships to those who wanted to study painting or music. There were so many other

The Wedding

Crowned and enthroned

After the ceremony

With Princess Farahnaz in Baluchistan, Embroidered Dresses

fish to fry that no one even considered that side of life. I
have now managed to convince those concerned that the
artistic disciplines are as important as the others, and
now the young who want to become theatrical directors
or conductors are also eligible for scholarships. I hope,
too, that the Farah Pahlavi Foundation, which I have just
founded will be an added encouragement to the world of
the arts. The real need was for an organisation which
would devote itself body and soul to the cultivation of
knowledge.

Indeed, it is becoming increasingly urgent because, if
we continue to develop at our present speed, we shall
soon be an industrial nation. It would, of course, be
absurd to deny the great benefits of progress: employment, education, hygiene, well-being, a higher standard
of living, but one would have to be blind not to see the
dangers. There will be pollution, families will be scat-
tered, people will no longer have time to concern themselves with their soul or to heed their neighbour. They
will become materialist and self-centred. Now, these
failings of the consumer society do not exist in the
developing countries because, the poorer people are, the
more closely they live together and the greater their
human qualities. How can this feeling of brotherhood be
preserved in a nation which seeks to become increasingly modern? How can we avoid the faults of the
nations which have preceded us on the road to indus-
trialisation?

One is almost tempted to preserve the poor little villages as they are in order that there may continue to exist
real human beings who care for one another. We tell
ourselves that our most urgent need is to protect them
from the folly of the world and a rapid increase in their
material wants. We see them at the entrance to their
tents, so peaceful and so proud, so noble and so generous in their poverty, contemplating the immensity of the
desert, heeding the seasons and the courses of the stars,
free. And one is overcome by a feeling of panic, imagin-
ing them throwing themselves frantically into the fatal
spiral of greed: no longer living, but working like

machines to buy a concrete house, and after the house, a car, then a refrigerator and a television set, and then finding satisfaction only in the roar and smoke of America, an apartment in Paris, a villa in Greece, a private yacht . . . their soul quite forgotten. Could it be that a high standard of living and quality of life are irreconcilable? I like to think they are not and to work for a new society in which one can build the future without losing respect for the virtues of the desert dweller.

4
What makes a Persian?

'What makes a Persian?' wondered Montesquieu. What are the characteristics and traditions which constitute 'Iranity'? It is difficult to say. The Iranians are a very diverse people so perhaps a separate definition is needed for every one of them. But they do have in common a past tradition of culture, science and literature which has remained very much alive, even among the most illiterate. There is not a peasant, buried in his hamlet, far from any school, who cannot recite a poem by Hafez or Saadi. The Iranians need poetry. Indeed, the oral tradition has kept history alive more effectively than all the books: Darius and Cyrus, our great Kings, are a part of our daily life, they are members of the family.

Perhaps it is this perennial quality which has preserved intact the virtues of hospitality, good manners and courtesy so special to the Persians, which bears no resemblance at all to good breeding as it is taught in the West. That which, to a European, may appear excessively courteous or even obsequious, is for us merely a natural expression of affection, deference or admiration, and marks the very great respect which the Iranian has always had for others. Intelligent, if he will take the trouble, he is also capable of being an excellent worker—but in some parts of Iran the heat is so great, the sun so oppressive that it is understandable if the people who live in such places sometimes lack zeal. But despite the harsh climate, the Iranian is always very gentle, very human, very kind. In the smallest village, the simplest

83

people will, by their welcome, their charm, their unspoiled character, remind the disillusioned town-dweller of the values his forbears knew how to cultivate.

It must be said that Iran is situated at a geographical crossroads and, throughout history, others have sought to control it. Unfortunately it was, long ago, the favourite route for the barbarian invasions. So our history is not free from bloody episodes. These upheavals split up the country into several hundreds of tribes, more or less nomadic, and armed to the teeth. There was a time when brigandage reigned supreme, when, at nightfall, each valley became a veritable death-trap. There were few roads and to travel along them without being attacked was almost a miracle.

A century ago, Iran was the prey of foreign influences which again divided it. The King no longer had any real power, he had to consult the British or Russian ambassadors before taking the smallest decision, nor had he any army worthy of the name. This was the situation in which my husband's father, Reza Shah, found it and, from this anarchy, he re-made a nation. With an iron hand, he reunited the tribes and began the task of restoring to his country an awareness of its past greatness. He was accused of severity, he was feared, but at the time, this was necessary and sometimes, even today, there are some who think: 'If only Reza Shah were still here, people would not be so irresponsible.'

When he had a bridge built, the engineer had to stand beneath it on the day of its inauguration as the stone-laden lorries crossed to test its strength . . . In Teheran today, it unfortunately happens from time to time that blocks of flats built in haste crumble about the heads of their inhabitants. If the architects had been obliged to live in them, this kind of accident would certainly have been avoided . . .

That was the way of Reza Shah, who began to rebuild Iran and restore to the Iranians their dignity. His Ministers had to walk several steps behind him. That seems strange to us now, but sometimes people think he was right, for if one is too kind to others, they often take liberties. They would trample over you to make sure of being in the photograph. However we evolve, a certain reserve must be maintained.

But, to return to the character of the Iranians. If they have sometimes been cruel, it is because circumstances have forced them to be so. Everyone is capable of cruelty in defence of his life. I myself would describe the Iranian as something of a grumbler: it is in his nature. He is capable, in a burst of bad temper, of criticising every-thing in his country, but should a foreigner begin to do the same in his presence, he would never stand for it and would immediately say the opposite. Sometimes I grumble myself, I criticise, and when my husband reproaches me for it, I tell him: 'Think of me as symbolis-ing the Iranian grumbler!'

However, a good grouse from time to time does not prevent a realisation and appreciation of all that has been done for the country. It can be felt in the trust which the people express to their King when they see him, whether in town or in the provinces, in the villages or in the letters he receives. What we need is not bad temper just for the pleasure of it, but a sense of responsibility and the sug-gestion of solutions to the problems which provoke our grumbles. It is always very easy to criticise others and to see, as they say here, the piece of straw in your neigh-bour's eye without noticing the tree-trunk in your own!

Iranians are often inclined to scepticism as a result of all the misfortunes which have befallen them in the course of their country's history, whether it be accidents of climate, the hazards of politics or the invasions which have ravaged their soil. Politicians have made them so many unfulfilled promises, foreigners have so exploited them that they find it difficult to believe in anything. But trust is being re-born, the reforms are so self-evident that they do not permit of doubt. However, Iranians must never again be deceived for they would revert to mistrust and, like a relapse in any illness, it would be far more difficult to find a remedy the second time around.

The danger does exist. In Iran, there are, for example, poor areas, shanty towns, where the people live in very difficult conditions. It is two years since I myself asked the Government to send an investigating committee to the spot to suggest measures to remedy the poverty and then to make me a detailed report. But these problems are very difficult. They cannot be solved in a day and I am sure some people, therefore, think that I am unaware of what is going on in the south of Teheran. That is why I am so anxious to prod people into developing a sense of responsibility, an acceptance of work and thought for others. It is an education which must be begun in the schools and cultivated in the bosom of the party so that each individual may become truly aware that he is a member of a united society which it is his duty to serve.

But this unity does not exclude diversity and the variety of customs among the tribes of Iran, if they continue to live in peace and friendship, is still one of the attractions of our country. There are the Qashquais of the Mountains of Fars; the nomads of Baluchestan, whose life is rigorous because of the climate; the Bakhtiaris; the Lurs of Lorestan; the Kurds on the frontier of Iraq; the Shahsavan; the mongol-like Turkomans with their slanting eyes, who live in the rich, green regions bordering the Caspian Sea. They are magnificent horsemen, who ride from their very earliest years, very colourful nomad warriors who live in their *yourtes* of felt and wear tall hats of astrakhan.

I find the life of the nomads fascinating and dream of being able, one day, to travel a few stages with them at the usual pace of their caravans. For them, too, things are changing: schools welcome their children when they take up their winter quarters and then, when they set out again across the deserts, teachers from the Army of Knowledge go with them, taking mobile libraries. Midwives and doctors from the Army of Health follow, too. The standard of education among them is, incidentally, very high. The percentage of nomad scholars at university is much higher than from settled homes: eight or nine out of ten. Some are sent to America or to Europe to study . . . Indeed, some nomads are immensely rich. They travel with refrigerators run on petrol, high-fidelity tape-recorders, portable television sets and their tents lack none of the comforts in the stone houses of the middle-class townsfolk who watch them go by.

It would take too long to name here all the tribes, branch tribes, clans or families which make up the Iranian mosaic. Whatever their number, they are united by three very strong ties: the monarchy, Islam and Iranity, which influence every moment of their lives. Our New Year is a tradition older than Islam, but the Koran and the portraits of our Imams always have a place in it. The ceremony of the last Wednesday of the year, when we jump over fire, goes back to the Zoroastrans. Our months bear the names of the Mazdean angels, but we use four calendars: according to the Hegiran calendar, which is in solar months, we are in the year 1356; according to the western calendar, it is 1977; according to the historic Iranian calendar, we are in 2536; according to the Mohammedan lunar calendar, it is 1397. Without a doubt, our culture and way of life are largely Islamic—we are very devout Shiite Moslems—but how we like to repeat in our speeches the precept of Zoroaster: 'Think well, act well, speak well!'

The perennial nature of our traditions, the ever-living presence of the institutions of our past, made it possible for us to celebrate at Persepolis, on 15 October 1971, the two thousand and five hundredth anniversary of the Persian Empire.

It was an outstanding occasion in the history of Iran and we decided to mark it with splendid celebrations. Twenty-five centuries of continuity for a nation, a people, a monarchy, is, without a doubt, unique in the world. For us, it was also a not-to-be-missed opportunity of making known the Iran of yesterday and the Iran of today, of showing the world the greatness of its past and the immense possibilities of its future. At Persepolis, Cyrus had known how to create a setting for peace and friendship. We wanted to follow his example and I think we succeeded. We invited a large number of Heads of State and I am sure that those who came spent there a few days they will never forget.

Apart from the historical interest, the success of these celebrations was ensured by what I consider the most important of all contributions: a wonderful team spirit. The Iranian has always been something of an individualist but, for those few days, everyone understood the importance of the event for their own country and all—be they chauffeurs, workmen, hotel workers, ladies-in-waiting, Ministers, Court officials—leaned over backwards to ensure that all would go well and that the guests should be well received. I saw Ministers carrying suitcases and ladies-in-waiting (some of them chosen from among my friends to attend the wives of the Heads of State) who would, if need be, have even ironed the guests' shirts. Everyone forgot his rank and devoted himself to serving. As for the workmen, they toiled ceaselessly right up to the dawn of the great day. In Iran, things are often left until the very last minute. People dawdle and dawdle and then, when time has almost run out, work like mad and, in some miraculous way, everything is ready when it is needed.

In the magnificent setting of Persepolis, sixty splendid tents were put up to receive our guests. They were furnished with every comfort and set out along avenues bearing the names of the five continents. Beside a huge reception tent were three others for the King, the Crown Prince and for me. It was an amazing sight and they have been left there for the interest of tourists and for the use of international conferences.

The Heads of State arrived one after the other. Each was greeted with his national anthem and the raising of his flag. It all went at considerable speed and great care had to be taken not to make a mistake. But the most difficult task of all fell to the Captain of the Guard of Honour. At each arrival, he had to present arms to the Monarchs, the Presidents and the Prime Ministers, proclaiming from memory their names and titles which, in some cases—especially for the Heads of State from Eastern Europe—were very long. And this valiant officer did it all without a single mistake. At the end, I went over to congratulate him and everyone in attendance on me did the same. Poor man, I fear that, as we say in Iran, we 'cast the evil eye on him' for, when he returned to his hotel, he was so tired that he walked straight into a plate-glass door . . . and broke his nose.

There was the Emperor of Ethiopia; the King of the Belgians and Queen Fabiola; the King and Queen of Denmark; the King and Queen of Jordan; the Grand-Duke and Grand-Duchess of Luxembourg; Prince Rainier of Monaco; the brother of the Emperor of Japan; the Sultan of Oman; the King of Lesotho, a small and ancient country in Southern Africa; all the Emirs from the Persian Gulf; the Prince of Spain, who has since become King, and Princess Sophie; Prince Philip and Princess Anne; Marshal Tito; M. Podgorny; the President of Hungary; President Ceausescu of Rumania; the brother of the King of Morocco; the President of Tunisia; the Vice-President of Egypt; President Senghor; President Moktar Ould Daddah of Mauretania; the President of the Sudan; King Olav of Norway; the President of Turkey; the President of Pakistan; Prince Bernhardt of the Netherlands; Prince Mikasa and Princess Yuriko of Japan; the daughter and son-in-law of the King of Afghanistan; Prince Nawaf of Saudi Arabia; Cardinal de Furstenberg, the Papal Envoy; the President of the Chamber of Deputies of Liberia; M. Wahlen, a former President of the Helvetic Federation; a representative of China; Vice-President Spiro Agnew of the United States; the Governor-General of Canada; the French Prime Minister, M. Chaban Delmas, and his wife, whom he had married only a very short time before; representatives of Italy and Germany; Mme Marcos of the Philippines; the King and Queen of Greece, in exile at the time, but still regarded as representing their country; the Crown Prince of Sweden, now King Carl Gustav; a member of the Royal Family of Thailand; a representative of Portugal and many others besides . . . In addition to the Heads of State or their representatives, we had also invited a number of specialists in Iranian matters or great friends of Iran. Altogether, there must have been almost two thousand people.

There were, inevitably, certain small problems of protocol because the Heads of State were ranked according to their seniority in office and not according to the importance of their country. Perhaps that is what upset France. It was a pity. At Eisenhower's funeral, for example, General de Gaulle sat, in all humility, in the place protocol assigned him.

In Denmark, people, press and government had put pressure on the King and Queen not to come, but they came nonetheless, out of friendship for Iran and for my husband. Queen Juliana of the Netherlands, on the other hand, sent Prince Bernhardt alone to represent her. But there were not really any other problems of this kind and this Areopagus of heads of state from all the corners of the globe, created a unique gathering which could not, I think, be repeated elsewhere on another occasion. They met in a conciliatory, friendly atmosphere, from which political problems had temporarily, perhaps, been banished. Many of them were anxious to meet one another without it being known and, there, they could do so with ease, in the certainty that they ran no risk of indiscretion. They went from tent to tent, paying one another visits, inviting one another to small tea-parties, or informal talks and in the evening they all came together in an almost family atmosphere. They all found it as pleasant as it was entertaining. They were so numerous that my husband had to be up until two or three o'clock in the morning in order to spend time with his guests. I scarcely saw him.

The arrival of all these notable visitors proved to the people of Iran the respect felt by the world for their history, their civilisation and for the present position of Iran in the comity of nations. It became a source of great pride and joy to them. I myself was very tired. A year before, I had been asked to preside over the organisation of these celebrations and it had meant considerable work. I had also spent much time explaining, so that all might understand, the true meaning of the celebration and our reason for holding it on such a scale. Thus it was that during the days preceding the ceremonies, I received more than thirty journalists, spending hours and hours in conversation with them, in turn explaining, discussing, telling, defending, remaining calm throughout. It was exhausting.

At the same time, the final touches to all the details for the receptions needed continual attention. I was also very anxious to know what effect the ceremonies would have, what impressions observers would draw and what benefit they would bring us. There were already criticisms, unfortunately concerning minor points of detail. The essence of the occasion had not been seized and I told myself that it was perhaps partly my fault, that I could not have explained it clearly enough. Some petty articles were no more than lists of silly minor details: His Highness X had lost his suitcase; there was noise in the kitchen, and other equally silly comments. Some attacks were so petty that they ended by defeating their own purpose and rebounded in favour of Iran. But this accumulation of fatigue and anxiety meant that I was not really on my best form. For the first time in my life I had to take pills to sleep and others to keep me going during the day. I followed all the ceremonies like someone suffering from amnesia, seeing almost nothing. I was present at the procession but later, when I saw the film of these ceremonies, I noticed an enormous number of details that had escaped my notice at the time. I had but one thought: that all should go according to plan and that nothing untoward should happen.

Fortunately, there were some amusing small incidents to cause a fleeting smile to hide my anxieties for a moment. My birthday coincided with the celebrations and a French cook had brought a huge cake from Paris. When it arrived, the crown surmounting it was a little broken. The cook wept floods of tears. He had taken such pains in its preparation, had brought it so far, and now his work of art had been 'sabotaged'. And so, between a meeting with Marshal Tito and a discussion on Europe with the King of the Belgians, there was the little cook to be comforted, to be told: 'It does not matter, it will not show, it is splendid, very beautiful and you will see that it can easily be put right . . .'

Among all the details claiming my attention was my own wardrobe because I wanted it to represent Iranian workmanship. My day dresses were cut from traditional materials, printed by hand. For the first ceremony, I wore a long gown with the embroidery of Baluchestan, that province on the frontier of Pakistan, with its geometrical designs in contrasting colours thrown into relief by the thickness of the threads. Our tourists have since come to know it well. For the procession, my gown had the same embroideries, but all in shades of blue on a white ground. The little dress of my daughter, Farahnaz, and the waistcoat of my son, Ali Reza, who sat beside me, were of the same material. For the first dinner, it was a brocade of an entirely new design and on the second evening, I wore a gown printed with the famous wooden blocks of Ispahan.

For us, the festivities began with a ceremony at the tomb of Cyrus at which only Iranians were present. For the citizens of this country, it was very impressive for it recalled the policies of the greatest of our Kings. Carved on a cylindrical stone, history has handed them down to us. They were amazingly generous, for they already included the basic principles of the rights of man: all racial discrimination was forbidden, there was to be absolute freedom of religion and slavery was to be abolished. And that was two thousand five hundred years ago! All around, the great civilisations were building their historical monuments on the corpses of their slaves, but in the huge yards of Persepolis all the workers were free and received a just wage. What a source of pride for Iranians to see their present King pay homage to his far-distant predecessor, repeating without the least anachronism, a profession of faith which dated back twenty-five centuries! And what a lesson for us, after so many years, to persevere in the way of our ancestors!

Before us, on the edge of the desert, the tomb of Cyrus the Great was impressive in its stark simplicity. He had lived in the grandeur and luxury of Persepolis, he lay at rest in the silence and purity of the sands, but he seemed curiously present in our minds.

In the town, the stone friezes still show the long procession of ambassadors from the countries of the empire: Medes, Parthians, Scythians, Assyrians, Thracians or Babylonians, come to bring their offerings to the Persian monarch. Where but here should one seek inspiration for the great historical procession which Iran then set before the Heads of the nations of the world?

Our guests saw the armies of our entire history pass before them. Many hundreds of soldiers had grown beards and long hair to resemble faces in our bas-reliefs. The dress was reproduced with a fidelity that had its origin in ten years of archaeological studies. The war towers of the Achaemenians drawn by teams of buffaloes, the horses of the Parthians, the camels, the foot soldiers of the Seleucidae and Sassanian dynasties, impressive in their authenticity, advanced between the columns and lions of stone, to martial music played on the instruments of their period—the direct predecessors of their modern descendants, the Soldiers of the Revolution and the Legion of the Servants of Humanity created by the King to carry help to the stricken of the entire world.

It was impossible not to be moved and I wager a good number of our guests sometimes felt a sharp, tingling thrill. The undertaking was extremely difficult and the risks were legion that it might descend to circus or carnival level. But the emotion aroused by the march of history owed nothing to the spectacles of Hollywood or to the contrivances of Cecil B. De Mille. Everyone taking part knew what he was representing and felt deeply the ties which linked him to his glorious past. Then, at the end of the procession, the conviction of the Iranians themselves showed the world the effort we are making today and the promise of our future.

In any case, the programme for our guests was not exclusively concerned with reminders of our past. During their stay, they had every opportunity to see our present accomplishments, in agriculture as well as in industry. On the evening of the procession, there was the offical banquet which opened with a speech by the Emperor Haile Selassie, then doyen of the world's Heads of State but who has since died in circumstances of which we are all aware.

I remember a rather amusing anecdote from that evening: many of the guests having come without their wives, there were fewer women than men. It therefore so happened that Prince Bernhardt of the Netherlands, Prince Rainier of Monaco and Prince Philip of England were sitting next to one another. Prince Bernhardt speculated: 'I wonder why we have no women between us?' to which Prince Philip replied: 'Because we are the only male queens.'

The following morning, it was my sons who took breakfast to the Heads of State in their tents. There were little electric cars for the purpose and sometimes, for fun, the Crown Prince would drive them. When evening came, after a tour of Persepolis and Pasargades, dinner was less formal than the preceding day. There was a buffet of Iranian dishes and people sat at small tables, with Iranian dancing girls performing traditional dances among them. The Heads of State were very relaxed and in that warm-hearted setting were able to speak openly to one another—usually about politics, needless to say—but in light-hearted vein. In this way, some exchanges were certainly more fruitful than they would ever have been in the usual bi-lateral conferences, so learnedly prepared by the technocrats as to stifle all exchanges of opinion. Afterwards, there was another very attractive *son et lumière* which lasted until half-past-one in the morning. I knew all these programmes by heart, minute by minute, but suddenly, at about two o'clock, we were given a surprise: an improvised display of fireworks. I was vexed, fearing some of the Heads of State, awakened suddenly, might take fright at the unexpected flashes, instinctively mistaking them for some military attack. I was also very worried for all the animals: buffalo, horses, mules and camels stabled not far from the camp. I was afraid that, unnerved by the very loud noise, they would suddenly bolt, overturning everything in their way.

But in fact, everything went off very pleasantly and the coaches which took the Heads of State from Persepolis to Shiraz or Ispahan sometimes took on something of the feeling of children's holiday outings.

Naturally, representatives of all the groups and all the social strata of Iran: workers, peasants, university dons, students, deputies, were also present at the ceremonies, but there were, too, simultaneous programmes of popular festivals in all the towns and villages of Iran and the commemoration ended with a great sports festival which inaugurated Teheran's new stadium with its capacity for a hundred thousand spectators.

Even before the celebrations began, criticism, needless to say, was not spared us. True, the tents, the furnishings and some of the meals were not produced locally, but it has to be remembered that Iran is a newcomer in this field, and her capacities in it are limited. For ten years, we prepared the historical side of these ceremonies with minute care, undertaking much research, producing many studies and publishing books. The actual organisation was, therefore, left somewhat until the last moment. We were more concerned with the meaning of the event than with its practical details. Naturally, I would have liked everything to have been the work of Iranian craftsmanship and labour but it was not humanly possible for us to produce in the space of one year all those things which were quite new to our experience. It was necessary to call on France for technical help.

As for the famous hairdressers conjured up in the imaginations of some people--the Alexandres or the Caritas and their like—people refused to believe that we had not paid them to be there, that they had come of their own accord, for their own pleasure and their own publicity. Indeed, much space was devoted to the false eyelashes, the hair pieces and the beauty products they brought, as if these petty details had the slightest importance when one was dealing with twenty-five centuries of history! And since my gowns were entirely Iranian, they were—it goes without saying—never mentioned. Yet, if I had been dressed by Dior or some other great European fashion house, pages and pages would have been written about it.

And finally, the figures for our expenditure were inflated at will. In fact, they were no more unacceptable than those which nearly every country spends each year on their carnivals, their national days or other traditional ceremonies.

It is, nonetheless, extraordinary that for an anniversary celebrating twenty-five centuries, we should be denied the right to mark the occasion with festivities symbolising their immense national importance. All the more so since most of the money we spent that year was not thrown uselessly away: the hotels, the roads, the tents remain and are still in full use. Furthermore, electricity was brought to many villages for the occasion and we have built nearly three thousand schools. Who dares to say all that was useless?

From the point of view of public relations, it won us an immense press campaign which cost us absolutely nothing. If we had had to pay for all the films and all the articles about our country published during this period by the television companies and the newspapers of the entire world, it would have cost us millions of dollars!

This 'promotion exercise' was not long in bearing fruit: many indeed were those who, beforehand, did not even know where to find Iran on a map and who suddenly learned something of its history and geography. The ever-increasing benefits it has brought us in the field of tourism alone would justify all the expense of Persepolis.

Furthermore, as a token of our desire for peace and the continued tolerance of the Iranian people, we created the Cyrus Foundation which, from its very beginning undertook the entire charge of four children of every race—a small black child from Africa, a small Canadian Indian, a small Iranian white child, a small Japanese—from their first day at school until the end of their university studies. To spread the idea of friendship, fraternity and equality among all races and all nations, we wish, under the aegis of UNICEF or UNESCO, to widen this gesture so that children of the whole world can be brought up together.

No effort was too great, no undertaking excessive if it enabled Iran once again to keep her appointment with history . . .

5

Whether I am good or bad

Whether I am good or bad,
You must remain what you are;
Each of us will harvest
What we have sown.

A PERSIAN POEM

It was not really until 1973, thanks to what is usually known as the 'oil boom', that Iran really attained her rightful place on the world scene. For us, the consequences of this event were extraordinarily far-reaching: a successful end to the long struggle to defend the interests of the country and of the Iranian people and the realisation of all the dreams cherished since the moment oil was nationalised.

It is well known that Iran was among the first to nationalise this natural wealth. This was in 1951 and the consequences were not, at first, very helpful. For many years we were more or less boycotted by the great oil companies and it was impossible to sell our oil, even at a low price. This caused a great economic and political crisis marked by the doubtful manoeuvres of Mossadegh and the brief voluntary exile of the King in 1953. We had to wait for the departure of Mossadegh and the consolidation of the régime before the crisis could be solved.

It was, therefore, not until 1954 that Iran was able to conclude an agreement with the consortium of oil companies which brought a temporary solution to our problems. All the advantages lay with the consortium for, by the simple process of regularly increasing production, it was able to control the exploitation of the oil fields. But, by 10 July 1973, we had become sufficiently strong to negotiate a new agreement by which Iran took over complete control of its oil but guaranteed the companies that they would be able to have as much oil as they needed. Only then did Iranian oil really belong to the Iranians. But it was still not sold at a fair price. Then came the war of October 1973, the embargo and the readjustment of prices. The event caused a great outcry but it was only fair: the industrialised countries were no longer able to obtain for a derisory sum the commodity on which the supremacy of their economies is based.

The Iranians were rightly proud. Iran had shown her independence and this considerable contribution to her economy made it possible for us to take a great step along the path to development. In every field, we were now able to put into effect the very many projects which would ensure the early renaissance of Iranian society. We built thousands of miles of roads and rail, we built airports, we extended the telephone network throughout the country, erected schools and hospitals, dams for irrigation and electricity, petro-chemical works, steel and iron works and so on. In comparison with the past, we had an enormous supply of money, but to avoid a galloping inflation which would, sooner or later, have wiped out our progress, we had to be on our guard against spending it all inside the country.

Incidentally, I took advantage of this wealth to have the Government buy back from abroad some major collections of Iranian art. The return to the fold of these emblems of our rich past was an investment as profitable financially as it was sentimentally—and it did not, of course, involve any risk of inflation!

Through the intermediary of the World Bank, Iran has granted to the developing countries of Asia and Africa seven million dollars of long-term loans at very low rates of interest, and has also given two-and-a-half million dollars to the poorest countries of the Third World. This considerable aid to the most deprived nations shows plainly that we have not been selfish with our sudden wealth. Iran also suggested the creation of an International Fund in which the developed countries, the oil producing countries and the countries without natural resources should meet on an equal footing to determine together the true needs of the most deprived and try to provide for them.

The important thing now is to realise that oil must not be used simply as a direct source of heat, for the petrochemical industry derives hundreds of products from it, each of them tremendously useful. As the King says, oil is a noble product. It would be ridiculous to draw it off to the last drop just for heating, which can be equally well provided by gas, coal or electricity without any risk of their becoming exhausted and at much less cost, if the effort were made to switch to their use. Many people still look on oil as a convenience, yet it is well known that the reserves are limited. It is high time we concentrated on research into other sources of energy: the sun, the wind, water and the tides, every conceivable form of combustible material. I hope with all my heart that the work is undertaken speedily so that there may be the least possible dependence on nuclear power stations.

But instead of arousing an essential awareness of the vital problem posed by the eventual exhaustion of oil supplies, many people have been incapable of any reaction except a negative one to the readjustment of its price, just though it was. Many articles, many political speeches were over-quick to forget the years and years when the reserves of the Third World were exploited to the full, and became mere diatribes against OPEC. 'They are asking far too much. They are going too far. They have no idea of the economic problems it may cause in the western hemisphere. They will cause world-wide inflation. Those countries of the Third World who are not producers of oil will be the first to suffer . . .' and so on.

Reality was distorted, interviews with the King were edited, we were a very convenient scapegoat: 'Well, if you have material problems, it is because of them!' How wonderful to be able to load one's own sins on to someone else in this way. And it worked. For a while, if the weather was cold in Europe, and there was insufficient heating, people meeting an Iranian woman in an hotel or a shop would say to her: 'Yes, it is your fault that we are cold! You are used to warmth in your country. Well, because of you, we are unfortunately unable to heat our hotels . . .' The poison bore fruit and the least domestic problem was blamed on the oil producing countries. What a godsend for the governments!

But fortunately, even in oil-importing countries, there were impartial, practical people, university dons, journalists or economists, who had studied the facts and considered we were justified. Unbiased scientific articles, supported by soundly-based statistics and graphs, upheld our action. And many ordinary people, too, those who had learned in the course of their own work to decide what was fair in the matter of prices, were sympathetic to Iran despite the problems which the 'boom' might be provoking in their own country.

Why was there such a widespread refusal to tell the truth about the price of oil? Quite simply because, despite its rise, it was not the producing countries who garnered the biggest profits. The price at which we sell our oil is, in fact, only a very small fraction of what western consumers pay to fill the tanks of their cars or those of their central heating systems. What does cost them dear, apart from the refining, is the enormous profits made by the big oil companies on transport or storage, as well as the taxes imposed by importing countries, taxes which are often far higher than the price of the oil itself.

Logically, a rise in the price of crude oil on the Persian Gulf should not even be noticeable to the man in the street in France or England—or if it is, only infinitesimally. But that is not the case. Every readjustment decided by OPEC has repercussions, it is multiplied five, six, seven times, sometimes even tenfold. For that, we are in no way responsible, but it is always the easiest of excuses to pretend that it is our fault.

But we do not harbour resentment and, in addition to

the considerable aid we have given the countries of the Third World, have invested very great sums to help western economies which are sometimes in difficulties. For us it was natural, human, for we do not wish to build Iran at the expense of others. It was not done in any spirit of misplaced pride or feeling of superiority. We thought it right to do so. We must help one another and, according to circumstances and possibilities, we must take it in turn to give and to receive.

Yet, through some inexplicably mean treachery, there are those who have been pleased to treat us as *nouveaux riches*. As if we did not have behind us centuries of history and civilisation to preserve us from such an attitude. While we were building Persepolis, in America and a great part of Europe there were only barbarians and savages living in mud huts. Generosity has always been an Iranian characteristic. In the very depths of Baluchestan, the peasant with few worldly goods is ready to share his bread and salt with the traveller from wherever he may come and without asking anything in exchange. Is he to be called *nouveau riche*? No, this great dignity in deed and attitude has never owed anything to money and I hope will never be spoiled by money. We have not sought to diminish others in order to appear great and we have no need to humiliate in order to assert ourselves. Sometimes, we ourselves have received help in certain difficult periods. But then the photographers were there and poor little children had to pose beside bags of flour or cases of powdered milk. No gift went unpublicised and when given even the slightest thing, we had, for the gallery, to make a show of sycophantic gratitude and to be profuse in our thanks. When the situation was reversed and we, in our turn, were able to render service to the most deprived, we never asked anyone to do that.

Clearly, we can no longer continue to distribute money here and there in the same way. We did so while we could, but since then, the market for oil has for some time been shrinking. We have sold less of it than we hoped, our revenues have dropped and that raises a few small budgetary problems. We must tighten our belts a little. But it is not serious. Whatever losses we may have suffered, the economies in the use of energy achieved by industrial countries are a sign that the world is beginning to show signs of sense. Almost everywhere, there is a determination to fight the malady of our day: waste. This example must be followed, at national level as well as by individuals. But we are having difficulty in making this understood, for Iranians always have a tendency to make more than is needed. It is a part of their tradition of hospitality. If they invite ten guests, they prepare food for twenty! They light twelve lamps where three would do. I myself, walking through the Palace, am always turning off lights.

But what is much more serious for us is the soaring prices of the goods we import. Some have increased one, two or even five hundred per cent. So, what else can we do but increase the price of oil? Yet, if we do so, there is a shrill outcry! People want everything to be unilateral: 'I am increasing the price of my product, but you must not increase yours. I will buy things cheaply from you, you must buy from me at a higher price!' It is not possible. Through close collaboration, a just balance has to be found and we must each of us control ourselves as much as we try to control others.

Oil is Iran's most important resource. For years and years we were forced to sell it, like jumble, for a paltry sum. We want it paid for, in future, at its proper value. It is our right and we shall try to make it respected. We have need of it to develop our industries and our agriculture, to promote education and social well-being, to help us progress. Otherwise, how are countries like ours expected to live? By agriculture? Desert, rocks, mountains and lack of water: that is the lot of our peasants if the revenues from oil do not enable us to build dams, dig wells or desalinate sea-water. We are criticised if any of our people are undernourished or go barefoot, if the rate of infant mortality or illiteracy is higher than in Europe but if we try to remedy these things by turning to best account our most important natural source of wealth, we are criticised again! Twenty or twenty-five years hence, the oil will be exhausted. How will the Iranians live then? That is our worry, that is the danger we are trying to avoid. But OPEC is being turned into a monster whose aim is to make the rest of the world miserable. We are accused of being the sole cause of worldwide inflation. Yet the price of corn is rising, cement is rising, sugar is rising, industrial products are rising at a rate which makes the ten or fifteen per cent rise in the cost of oil seem derisory. In truth, it is the economic system itself of all these countries which is at the root of inflation. It is an internal problem, in which oil accounts for scarcely one per cent.

Some forget that they owe their position or their present comfort to the national resources of the colonies they controlled for centuries in Africa, Asia or elsewhere. That is only a bad memory which they have banished. But people must begin to understand that the world cannot go on in this way, with so many differences between one country and another, one continent and another. It is inadmissable that in some nations, food and money are thrown away while in others people are dying of hunger and lack the means to learn to read. Without a certain degree of joint responsibility, we shall never know peace. Some are aware of this truth and work for a new world balance but others are completely indifferent to it. If it is suggested to them that they should share in an attempt to set some underdeveloped country on its feet, they reply: 'Let them manage as best they can.' They scarcely consider them human beings, these gaunt, ragged creatures in whose veins flows, nonetheless, the same blood as in their own. They are as accustomed to their own comforts as to the poverty of others. How can they be made to understand that every man, whether he be red, black or yellow of skin, is their equal?

Considering themselves superior and, furthermore, above criticism, these people take unto themselves the right to judge all others. They are the sole custodians of the great principles. The slightest suspicion is a pretext for trial and condemnation. And so, for some time now, whenever Iran is mentioned, the only point which interests the Western press is the rights of man and the fact that such organisations as Amnesty International have chosen us as their favourite target.

But why Iran and why now, suddenly? It is very curious that the attacks always begin, as if by merest chance, when problems have arisen concerning oil. There is a noticeable coincidence between student demonstrations in Teheran or elsewhere and discussions about the readjustment of the price of oil. The attention of many powers is focused on Iran and it is a magnet for vast interests. Let us not speak of the Communists. We enjoy very good relations with the Eastern countries and the Soviet Union, both politically and economically. But, at heart, it is still their ideal that Communism should establish itself throughout the world and they will do all in their power, by one means or another, to see that it spreads in Iran. At the same time, our oil policy is far from satisfactory to all other governments. Some great multi-national companies, which have enormous power in the press and in various political and financial circles, use every means at their disposal to bring us to our knees.

To this, must also be added jealousy. Only yesterday, Iran was a practically unknown country. People had a rough idea of its whereabouts in Asia, they knew by repute the Shah of Iran, Persian carpets, caviare and Persian cats. That was all. Now, here is that backward, underdeveloped country beginning to achieve reforms, starting a progressive revolution and, in any case, showing itself more revolutionary than many of the régimes which pride themselves on being so. Furthermore, its Head of State begins to speak loud and clear, to argue the price of oil and, in so doing, even influences the policies of other countries! Iran develops rapidly, Iran becomes rich, buys all it wants—almost—begins to express an opinion, conducts a policy which is truly national and independent, has its say on the international scene. There is no doubt that this does not please everyone. The

105

West has always looked on the Asiatic or African countries from the height of its own grandeur and is unwilling to admit that 'this little country, suddenly, dares to formulate opinions on what we should do'.

And then, the Iranian Head of State declares: 'It is not the fault of the oil that your economy is failing. Your political system is unsound. Furthermore, your problems prove that your democracy is not really an ideal form of democracy. We, therefore, have no reason to imitate it'. For people who have, for centuries, thought they knew everything, that their way was the best, that it was their duty to dictate their law to all, and that others understood nothing, had nothing to contribute, it was a serious accusation. And so, instinctively, as soon as some small kernel of hostility towards Iran makes its appearance, other currents of opinion, whatever their natural divergences, unite with it and the spark becomes a blaze.

Iran is a country which arouses interest by reason of its natural wealth. Its geographical position is so important that it is the subject of more attention than other countries which, also, are producers of oil. Formerly, our country was dominated by a group of foreign influences and certain Iranian politicians joined this game, thus clearly making possible all kinds of manipulation.

Today, Iran refuses to be the servant of this or that great power. This arouses displeasure. And of course, when a country displeases the great powers, they try to sow enough trouble to instil fear into the rebel. They whisper: 'We are still the strongest. If you try to move, remember that we are watching you and that we can cause you harm!' And they can do this because we have no means of defending ourselves. Neither our press nor our television is comparable with theirs. And then, there is this international terrorism which manifests itself almost everywhere. God knows why all these young people take part in it. They do not even have any precise ideas and one is left with the impression that, after a while, they forget why they took that road. They get excited and imagine they are revolutionaries. They think they can change the world, they sow death and call it self-expression.

But what people do not know is that when someone has something worth saying, it is not forbidden in Iran to criticise or to be against this or that aspect of politics, so long as it is not expressed through violence, murder or crime. If these young people have a point of view to offer, they may do so and, if this opinion is a reasonable one, the idea will be followed up, will convince an increasing number of people and, perhaps, one day reach fulfilment. If there are any who think that some aspects of the King's policies—agrarian reform, the allocation to the workers of twenty per cent of the profits and forty-five per cent of the shares in factories, or the nationalisations—are mistaken, these are points which can be discussed and if the majority of the public agrees, changed. It cannot be said that it is forbidden to discuss the Government's policies. If one has a good point, why not? But, naturally, without going so far as to shout 'Down with the King!'

However, to criticise the bloodless revolution is to criticise the King. But these few groups of terrorists which have been formed in Iran offer no alternative system, they simply want to wreak havoc and create chaos. They are given guerilla training in certain foreign countries so that they may come and set bombs here—or even elsewhere. If they even had a common political objective—but they have not. Of this we have proof. They are caught up in this or that subversive movement, without any human ideal, without any coherence, apart from the intention to spread disorder. They urge themselves on, saying 'So-and-So began with twelve people'. They have only one idea: to oppose, and if it should be the innocent who suffer, well, that's too bad.

In recent interviews given to the Western press, the King admitted that, by European standards, there are about three thousand political prisoners in Iran. But when people are in touch with international groups whose purpose is subversion, when they collect terrifying arsenals of weapons and plan to kidnap or to kill, what else is there to do but to shut them away to prevent them doing harm? If the French police had captured the notorious 'Carlos', would they have freed him out of respect for his 'political' opinions? And the members of the Baader Meinhof gang: why these crimes and these suicides? 'Let those who seek lice in our hair begin by washing out their own!' If someone distributes pamphlets some night in the university or on the street, we allow him to do so. It is *terrorism* that we are fighting.

In that case, people will say to me, why this figure of three thousand, and why do so many of the young resort to violence? Alas, I fear the answer is very simple: in our singleminded preoccupation with development, we have neglected our public relations, we have not learned to present attractively the tremendous progress we have made. And so, within the country as well as abroad, some people are unaware of it and the less intelligent, spurred on by ill-disposed propaganda, take advantage of the slightest injustice to condemn the régime and to rebel. Some travel abroad: they see America, Europe, another world. Is it really free from all discontent? But they think that if Iran is not like New York, Los Angeles or Paris, it is the fault of the régime. They are quite unable to realise that it takes time and patience to modify existing structures, that it is not a particularly easy thing to do and that to achieve it, we need their help.

Our detractors claim exorbitant figures: forty thousand political prisoners, or even one hundred thousand! Yet journalists have visited the prisons, interviewed prisoners they thought dead or paralysed by fearful tortures. But their reports were never published. Doubtless, they were not sufficiently spicy. Only news items unfavourable to Iran are worthy of the front pages. Intellectuals do not like favourable comment.

I do not claim that we are blameless in certain cases, nor that we have never made mistakes, for there is no country in the world in which the police are entirely beyond reproach and gifted with sufficient self-control to meet all situations without resorting to violence. What is to be done with someone who has put a bomb in some public place, threatening dozens of human lives and who will not confess where he has put it? But we do not know how to present these things and give them the necessary publicity. The police publish very laconic press statements: 'Shots were exchanged between the police and the terrorists. Two terrorists were killed', which obviously gives the impression that there was no desire to take them alive. I have spoken to those concerned. When such a struggle arises, why not immediately summon television cameras, photographers, journalists to bear witness to our good faith?

I was in Amman during November when terrorists besieged an hotel. It was all filmed by television cameras; people could hear the machine guns, see the mounting flames and the wounded emerging. It aroused sympathy for the parachutists and the special forces who attacked and killed or captured those terrorists. There, no one could doubt the facts. Another example of our maladroitness? A few days ago, a number of political prisoners were freed. One of them had tried to kidnap me with my son. He was shown on television reading a message thanking the King for his clemency. That should never have been shown in such a manner. Everyone will certainly have thought that his message was dictated whereas, in fact, he really had written it all himself.

But, having said this, we should remember that conceptions of liberty in industrialised countries and in developing ones are of necessity different. If, in France, freedom of expression has become a basic principle, in the province of Baluchestan it is seen differently . . . What the Baluchi want is to have enough to eat, to own land to cultivate, to receive medical care, to send their children to school, to submit their problems to the municipal councils. In a few years' time, it may be that the freedom of the press will have become of great importance to them, too, but for the moment it is really not one of their first priorities.

The people of the West would like to see all the countries of the world unquestioningly adopting their systems. But does the fact that they have chosen a certain way mean that it is necessarily the best? I wonder. The present failures of the industrialised countries, the social injustices and the corrupting vices of capitalist society do not seem to me to represent in any degree a success so unquestionable that one should have a right to hold it up as a model. We have no wish to imitate anyone. For us, the essential is that, one day, every Iranian should be able to take charge of his own destiny and that of Iran. Until we reach that day, we do not claim to be a democracy, only a country *working towards democracy*.

6
Seek not water, seek thirst

Seek not water, seek thirst
And springs will rise around thee.
MULAHVI

If problems are to be understood, it is not enough to read reports—the situation must be examined on the spot. Since my marriage to the King, I have travelled a great deal. It is without a doubt one of the most absorbing and constructive facets of my life. I have made numerous visits abroad but I have also travelled in my own country from one end to the other, gradually learning to know it.

I have been to places where no King or Queen has set foot for years and years. Places that have remained more isolated than others and are almost forgotten in the capital. One such place was Baluchestan, which I visited ten years or so ago. We went through tiny villages, very sparsely populated. The soil was well suited to agriculture, but the great problem was water. In truth, Iran was preoccupied with so many problems of development that investment in Baluchestan was not thought economically attractive. In one place, for instance; people wanted a cement factory built, but the experts replied: 'It is not possible, because it is not economic.' This annoyed me. It was the first of my journeys and I said: 'Then, of what use is it for me to visit these places if no attempt is to be made to solve the water problem, if it is not economic to do this or that? What is to become of these people?'

I asked for reports on the possibilities of irrigation.

111

Some declared that water could be found and, in fact, a private firm has drilled wells and created a really large model farm. Since then, much has been done to help the people in this region. In agriculture, it was necessary to begin at the very beginning. At first, it was impossible to build because the peasants did not even know the exact limits of their lands. They would say: 'My land goes from this tree to this stream.' The first step, therefore, was to define boundaries, then, little by little, we built clinics, hospitals, schools, farms and factories.

The inhabitants were touched to see me and received me warmly. I thought that in some villages I might not even be recognised, that they would not know who I was. I had been told that in some very remote places, people were still unaware that the Pahlavi dynasty had, fifty years earlier, replaced that of the Qadjar. Indeed, that would have seemed to me perfectly understandable among village people so far removed from all political life and all sources of information. But it was quite otherwise and I remember that, as I went through one small hamlet, a woman said to the policeman who was holding her back: 'Let me see my Shahbanou!' Now, 'Shahbanou' is a title which I am the first to bear—it was created for me.

Along my route, everyone knew exactly who I was. Our contacts were very natural and very direct. At first, I was rather worried about going into such poverty-stricken places but I found there people of such personality and elegance, despite the very harsh conditions of their lives, that I felt more like weeping for the lives led by people in Teheran rather than pitying the fate of the Baluchis, a people so proud and often so gay. Their costume has a rare beauty: embroidered kaftans in many colours, jewellery of gold and silver, the head-dresses of the women contrasting with the more sober elegance of the men in their baggy trousers and wide shirts gathered under tight waistcoats. Their most faithful companion, even today, is the camel which can endure the difficulties of long journeys and which the Baluchis adorn with their finest ornaments: ceramic pearls to bring good fortune,

Relaxing at the Villa
Suvretta

At the self-service
restaurant, Pahlavi
University, Shiraz, 1969

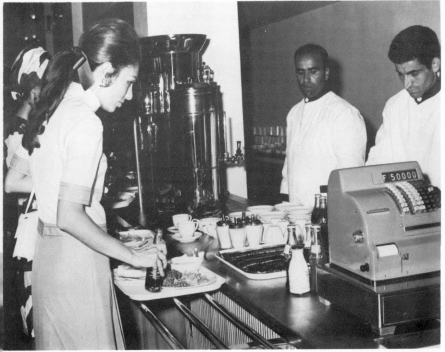

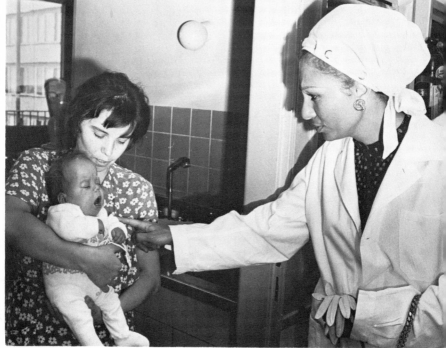

Opposite
Above opening an
exhibition in Turkey.
Below inspecting a
children's hospital,
Prague, 1977

The 2500th Anniversary of
the Persian Monarchy,
1971
Above: Being welcomed by
Iranian women
Below: Arriving at the site
of the tomb of Cyrus the
Great

The Shah and Shahbanou with their children: *left to right:*
Princess Farahnaz (born 1963), Crown Prince Reza (born
1960), Princess Leila (born 1970), Prince Ali Reza (born 1966)

medallions to protect against the evil eye, a profusion of gaily-coloured pompons and rugs. Silhouetted on the backs of their camels, their gaze as hard and dry as the climate of their region, their shoulder-length hair and long, thick moustaches, such are the last riders of Baluchestan. They invited me into their tents of palm leaves and, quite informally, I drank tea with their families.

In one of the small towns I visited, the poor Governor had no proper place for receiving guests, so he had to borrow mattresses from the consul of Pakistan . . . He went to great pains to prepare a room for me. In other places, there would be only one bathroom and in the mornings the entire delegation would have to take it in turn to make a hasty toilet . . .

Further south, we stopped in a wonderful port and I have dreamed ever since of it becoming a second Bay of Rio. It is called the 'Four Springtimes' because of the well-known mildness of its climate. There again, there were only very few inhabitants, only one large building. This did not seem to worry them. Their gaiety, despite their quite modest lives, made a deep impression on us.

Of all my journeys, that to Baluchestan remains one of my best memories. For me, it was not a matter of comfort, what made it stand out was my contact with the people. They felt not the least constraint and, thanks to their perfect, inborn hospitality and the simple manner in which they received me, I had a strong feeling that there were no barriers between them and me. During the journey, M. Alam, then Court Chamberlain, would no sooner see four or five trees than he would announce to me: 'Over there is a forest' . . . On the return journey, when we arrived at Bandar Abas, a rapidly-expanding port, we felt as startled—after all those little villages with such backward living conditions—as if we had suddenly landed in New York or Tokyo! Since then, there have been great changes in Baluchestan: the telephone, radio, television, roads and aeroplanes bring not only the roar of the outside world but also the means of development.

But there is not only Baluchestan. Our regions differ widely, and so do their needs. The purpose of my journeys, apart from personal contact with the people, is to draw the attention of the Government and relevant institutions to the urgency of certain human and material problems as described by those who live with them. From the capital of a country, it is impossible to get an exact idea of all that is involved.

In its own way, the desert, too, made a deep impression on me. I enjoyed strolling there in the evening after a busy day, looking at it, feeling it, absorbing its ineffable peace, the incomparable purity of the sky, contemplating nights when the stars seem to stretch down to the very earth. The boundless horizon, the silence, the pride of those who live there, the generosity of their welcome despite the hostility of the elements, all this makes the desert the most enchanted of all places. The great nomads who cross it are the last witnesses to an ancient order in which the rhythm of life, bound to that of nature, was without a doubt more human than that of today. Only ten years or so ago, one could still see in Teheran caravans of dromedaries with their elegant, unhurried gait. Their bells could be heard from afar. Their passing has become the nostalgic ghost of a beauty which has almost disappeared and which those who live in towns are now trying to recapture. An increasing number of Iranians, instead of spending their holidays in Europe, are taking family holidays in the region of Tabas or Bam. We are trying to develop our hotel accommodation and at the same time preserve the natural beauty of the areas so that we may encourage this new form of tourism which, in the jet age, keeps all Iranians in touch with one another and preserves their unity.

In the heart of the desert, in Kavir, I remember passing through an extraordinary little village. It was like another world: small houses made of earth, tiny courtyards surrounded by high walls to give shade, lanes with low roofs to give protection from the sun. It was very hot there in daytime and very cold at night. The women wore the *tchador*, the traditional veil, but it was checked, like tartan, in green and pink or brown and red, and woven by themselves. The people—it was so very remote from everything—were not very cultivated and had received no education at all. Yet everyone greeted me in verse! The addresses of welcome, the petitions, the least sentence was a poem. Every ten metres, a man or woman would come forward to recite the poem written in my honour. After reciting hers, an old woman of about eighty suddenly threw her veil over my head and, beneath its shelter, clasped me to her bosom and embraced me enthusiastically. My entourage stood aghast. In fact, she was insisting on demonstrating her affection but was unwilling to show her face to my escort or make her gesture in sight of the crowd. So she made this little improvised tent in order that she might be alone with me and clasp me to her heart. It was the village of poetry.

In another place which I thought enchanting, the inhabitants demanded modern buildings. How to explain to them that their little village was so pretty as it was, so special and so full of charm? 'What can anyone do with these ruins?' they would say. How could one make them understand that the coveted house of brick and steel could not be adapted to the climate of their region and that their traditional dwellings were infinitely preferable to any built like a box?

Near a similar village, we built a very modern clinic, too sophisticated in relation to the needs of the villagers. Psychologically, it deterred people. The women did not dare go into it. They were embarrassed to speak of personal problems, whether of hygiene or the education of children. One day, there was a breakthrough, the result of months of patient effort. Until then, I had been unaware of such difficulties. You have to be on the spot to know what action to take. What gives me great pleasure is when the peasants are aware of spiritual values, when they respect their art and want to preserve their traditions. Occasionally, one will indicate to me that the ancient tomb of some philosopher, poet or writer is in need of restoration, or another will point out that it would be a good thing to save a particularly beautiful caravanserai.

Still in the desert, while I was visiting a place which had not been originally included in the programme, someone came to invite me to visit the bazaar of Damghan. It was impossible, I really did not have the time, but he was so insistent: 'I beg of you, come, the people have spread carpets across all the streets, they await you and if you do not come, they will be terribly sad . . .' I could not refuse, I told myself that I might never pass that way again. I did not regret it: I met people of tremendous personality, the women were not in the least shy, not at all the kind to hide behind their menfolk, without a word to say for themselves. They told me all their problems in a most straightforward manner. I learned a great deal that day and it was well worth the detour.

During another of my tours through the villages, I saw a legless woman throw herself almost under the wheels of my car. The driver braked just in time and I got out. Whereupon, she threw herself into my arms and embraced me, trembling with emotion. She wept so much that speech was impossible.

I calmed her and asked her in a friendly manner: 'What can I do for you?' Her hands, too, were half paralysed but she managed to bring out from beneath her gown a piece of material on which she had embroidered the portrait of the Crown Prince: 'Although it was not easy for me to do this embroidery, I wanted to give it to you because I wrote to your office and you did not leave my letter unanswered. I want nothing, only to thank you. I think of you continuously.' It was very moving to realise that, ill as she was, she had risked her life, not to ask for something, but simply to show her gratitude to me.

Year after year, journey after journey, I return to Shiraz, each time with increased pleasure. 'The city of roses, of wine and of poets' is blessed with a very mild climate and very pure air. Is that why the people of Shiraz are so special? They speak Persian with a slight accent which enhances their natural poetry. And in the evenings, there they are, a rug under one arm and samovar in hand, settling themselves near a stream for a picnic and a conversation studded with quotations from Hafez or Saadi. In Shiraz, the tombs of our two great poets are for all of us, whether labourer or intellectual, places of pilgrimage and meditation. In other places, people honour military leaders, here they honour those who sang of love, of flowers and of birds. The town, with its cypresses and rose bushes, offers the visitor, after his desert crossing, the scent of its wonderful gardens and the shade of its peristyles supported by slender pillars of carved wood, and it recalls to each of us the past splendours of Iranian art. From blue-tiled mosques to bazaars bejewelled with agate and silver, moves the kaleidoscope of the coloured robes of the nomads bringing their *kilims*, those carpets woven in geometrical and contrasting designs which the West is learning today to appreciate. And, of course, when the falling night hides the delicate shapes of the roses, there arises the song of the nightingale and for a moment, over the cups of tea, words fall silent and give way to dreams.

The coming of the Festival brought the unfamiliar harmonies of contemporary music, but Shiraz, that admirable city of all inspirations, has the secret, as does no other place, of mingling the charms of the past with the pleasures of the future. She is not set in her literary and architectural past: her university is one of the most important in Iran and she has found a way of adding the industries so indispensable to her development and renewal, without any lessening of her ancient beauty. Shiraz is perhaps the model of expansion as we understand it in Iran, a source of well-being and progress, but respectful of our human values and traditions.

Each year, with the King, we go in pilgrimage to Meched, to the tomb of the Imam Reza. It is said that he grants prayers and multitudes of believers from Afghanistan, Pakistan and every part of Iran make their way to his tomb. Inside, it is wonderfully ornamented with mosaics and mirrors. The Iranians have always put all their love and their wealth into these religious centres.

117

It is a sanctuary of peace, of meditation and whenever I come, I am left alone there for at least five minutes so that, through prayer, my cares may be lightened and my courage renewed. Wherever I go, if there is a holy place, I make a point of visiting it first. I feel that in such places I make my peace with myself, and I always emerge strengthened and more serene. In Teheran one day, feeling rather depressed, I took my mother into a very small shrine not far from the Palace. We went in an ordinary car and wore veils to avoid being recognised. I went in and sat for a few moments. Only one or two other people came in, ordinary workmen, who did not in the least disturb my meditations. It was all that was necessary to enable me to go out again in peace.

By reason of my duties, I have made so many journeys from end to end of the five continents that it would be tedious to describe them all here. So I shall content myself with recalling a few isolated memories, either because I think them particularly significant or because they had a special meaning for me and return often to my mind during conversation or when looking through photograph albums.

In 1962, the King and I went on an official visit to the United States. I still knew very little about politics but I think that, in those days, the Americans knew as little about the internal affairs of Iran, our efforts and our problems.

However that may be, we were faced with many hostile demonstrations by students—or so-called students—both Iranian and American. As if by chance, they were to be found wherever we went. Even when we went privately to some restaurant, unannounced in the papers, they were there. Furthermore, while it is a rule in the United States that demonstrations, if they are authorised, should keep at a certain distance, these sometimes came to within a few feet of us. It was quite contrary to accepted custom. In California, during our first encounter with the demonstrators, they went so far that the people accompanying us were extremely embarras-

118

sed. A policewoman near me said to me with tears in her eyes: 'You are so kind, why do they do such things?'

However, it was my first journey to the United States and, apart from these unpleasant incidents, I found it very impressive. The skyscrapers of New York . . . indications everywhere that, here, one has reached the furthest point of progress. Everything is bigger, more vast, more powerful than elsewhere . . . As for the White House, our palaces seem very small in comparison. The protocol is much more sophisticated and all the details certainly more lavish, both in the decoration and in the furnishings and table settings.

In those days, my English was not fluent and I found it very difficult to understand the English of Lyndon Johnson, then Vice-President, with his very strong Texan accent. I commented on it to President Kennedy who roared with laughter and answered: 'Neither do we!' But Jacqueline Kennedy spoke French very well and came to my rescue when I was at a loss for a word. She was very pretty, taller and fairer-skinned than she appears in photographs.

I returned to the United States later on a private visit. Then, I was able to go about, visit the shops and enter restaurants undisturbed. One evening, with our Ambassador and some friends, we went to a night-club, not the dark kind with slow music but a discothèque with quick rhythms and numbers of young people. Some asked me to dance. It was certainly against all protocol but the atmosphere was so informal, had such a holiday air about it, that I could not refuse. And then, you know how the Americans talk, they coolly asked me:

'How is the Shah? Is he not here with you?'

'No. Who are you?'

'I am your friend.'

Or a girl would come up to me, say 'Hello' and tell me: 'I saw your interview and found it terribly interesting.'

It was a very pleasant evening.

On that same visit, we went from Los Angeles to San Francisco by car. We stopped once at a restaurant by the roadside. The owner knew about my visit from television and the newspapers and came towards us—I was with a woman friend—saying quite unaffectedly: 'Honey, I don't know which of you two is the Queen and I would like to give her a small present.'

We visited the incredible world of Hollywood—it is perhaps a pity to penetrate the actors' secrets for it destroys some of the illusion—and I met Cyd Charisse, Ginger Rogers and Danny Kaye for whom I have a great admiration. He is an excellent actor, who has done a great deal for UNICEF and has organised numerous soirées for the benefit of deprived children. I watched the making of parts of the film during which Marilyn Monroe died. Then, there was the amazing Disneyland. Walt Disney was a wonderful man, no child in the world will contradict me on that point. In any case, only in America is it possible to achieve such prodigious success. Another example of someone who began with nothing but worked extremely hard is President Nixon. But, having said that, Watergate has shown that the fall can be as spectacular as the rise. The Americans then, in their crisis of confidence, showed their need for leadership.

But in all my journeys, the most magnificent welcome I ever received was, paradoxically, in a totally different world: the People's Republic of China. It was in 1972, the first official visit I made on my own. M. Hoveyda, who was Prime Minister at the time, accompanied me, but in the absence of the King, it was I who represented Iran. It was also the first time for many a long year that Iran had met China. Princess Fatemeh had been there on a private visit, as had also Princess Ashraf, but this visit marked the resumption of diplomatic relations between us. And China attached great importance to the renewal of these contacts. The reception was, of course, not for me, but for my country. As I left the plane, I could not believe my eyes: the marching, the bands, the dances, the many-coloured streamers and paper flowers . . . I thought everything had been concentrated at the airport and that there would be nothing further, but on the Tien An Men Square, the main square of Peking, there was even greater excitement.

We arrived in open cars, with M. Chou En-lai, whom I have always greatly admired. He is one of those beings who, when they die, seem irreplaceable. He was a man of discretion and elegance, who moved and spoke with a certain distinction. And then, he had done so much for China. He was a truly likeable and wonderful man.

In the open car, we drove for mile after mile through streets lined on both sides with crowds of young people. There were songs and dances and cries of 'Long Live the Queen! Long Live the Empress!' The Iranian journalists, who had arrived before us, had met certain difficulties. But at the very first official dinner, M. Chou En-lai mentioned in his speech the friendly relations which existed between Iran and China and the atmosphere changed for everyone. Everywhere they went, the journalists and diplomats were always received with smiling hospitality. Some observers declared that, apart perhaps, from the reception offered to Ho Chi Minh, it was the warmest welcome every given on the street to foreigners.

It occurred to me that for this people, who had always heard the Emperor and Empress of China blamed for all their misfortunes, to be shouting 'Long Live the Empress!' in Chinese was somewhat paradoxical. But they were all smiles. And no diplomatist could recall official dinners, usually marked by oratorical rivalry or angry walk-outs, ever being so pleasant and relaxed.

M. Hoveyda is a wonderful travelling companion, for he is very cultivated and has a great sense of humour, so we had wonderfully interesting discussions each evening about all we had seen and the surprise we had felt. We teased our Minister for Cooperatives, who thought the Chinese system excellent and wanted to adapt it for Iran.

It is incredible how clean and industrious the Chinese are. On their streets there is not a speck of dust, nor a scrap of paper to be seen and, in the countryside, not even the tiniest corner of land is left uncultivated. They may not have many clothes, but everything they wear is spotless. Nowhere did we see anyone dirty or in rags. It is perhaps rather dreary to have everyone dressed

121

exactly alike—only the small children and now, the girls, are allowed a little colour—but at least it looks neat. In Iran there are families and regions where the people are certainly far richer and have many more clothes but their appearance still gives an impression of shabbiness, or lack of care. It is a matter of habit, discipline, an attitude of mind. The little boys are very amusing: their trousers have an opening at the back so that they can satisfy the needs of nature wihout having to undo buttons. It is very strange.

The Chinese people are of course communist and therefore their museums show scenes from the life of the Emperor in his splendid palace, with all his gold plate, set next to harrowing paintings of villagers dying of hunger. But when I visited these museums, my guides showed truly oriental discretion by walking past these tableaux so that I should not feel they saw the least connection between an Empress of the old China and me. In another communist country I visited, I was, on the contrary, told with some satisfaction: 'This is where the King was arrested . . .' It was also the first time the Forbidden City had been opened and we were able to visit all the palaces, a privilege previously denied the public.

The Chinese go to extraordinary lengths in order to economise. For example, if there are three buttons on men's suits, one day they will decide that, in future, there will be only two. Just imagine the number of buttons saved . . . When they wanted to eliminate insects, the Chinese took fly-swats and killed them. After a few days, hardly any were left. They do everything together, in a way which is most impressive and at the same time intimidating. All the cultural programmes have revolutionary themes and their number is fairly limited. In China, there is iron discipline even for the children. Some very young ones had formed a traditional orchestra of ancient instruments which they played very charmingly. When they were congratulated, they always said it was nothing, that they ought to do better, that it was not enough. They all said the same. If you told one:

'You have made a pretty drawing,' the reply would invariably be: 'Yes, but I should try to do better.'

The manner in which they have pursued their development and the way in which they work are amazing. It could not be done elsewhere, but one must admire them because they have abolished want, poverty, epidemics and famine. What is less admirable is the dragooning of all these very small children. It must be impossible for any of them to develop freely as individuals. They all have to follow a set path. From their most tender years, their education is revolutionary and everything must have some connection with the revolution, works of art like everything else. To see these little ones of three or four years of age singing songs with clenched fists outstretched is rather frightening.

I visited a hospital where acupuncture was used to produce anaesthesia. It was very remarkable but later, when it was being discussed, our guides said that such-and-such a doctor had not dared to use it before but that, after reading the *Thoughts of Mao*, had had the courage to do so . . . Then, when we spoke of acupuncture itself, we were told that there was no precise or theoretical explanation of what happened and someone said: 'The masses should be consulted so that the problem may be solved.' That, too, was rather frightening.

All that the Chinese do is done for their country. In the factory, the workers repeat: 'We work to serve our country.' We saw an acrobatic entertainment and, at the beginning, the tight-rope walkers said: 'We do this to develop our bodies so that we may be strong to defend our country.' The people have little access to information by radio or television; there are not many newspapers and the only news is that which comes through the Party. Everything is divided into revolutionary committees for the town, the suburb, the house, the whole region . . .

Having said this, some aspects of China are very attractive. I remember Hang Chow, a most beautiful town studded with gardens and lakes, a place of enchantment. Legend has it that an angel was looking at

Paradise in a mirror, that the mirror then broke and one of the pieces fell to earth at Hang Chow. Chinese civilisation is extraordinary and has remained so, even if only in the field of gastronomy: at dinner, we would be offered perhaps twenty-two different dishes, garnished with vegetables moulded into the shape of birds. When it was time for the speeches, or toasts, the Chinese, being unable to pronounce either 'r' or a final 'h', always called me 'Falahe'.

Always at my side was a very amusing girl who acted as my guardian angel. She was an officer, but each time I asked her rank, she would smile without replying. It is impossible to know military ranks in China. There are neither stars nor rings to distinguish a Captain from a Sergeant, a Colonel from a General and I wondered how they made the distinction among themselves. It is perhaps this minor mystery which characterises them best.

In any case, since this visit, we have remained on excellent terms with China and, more than any other country in the world, she has always unequivocally and firmly upheld the policies of Iran. The first time she took part in any of the Olympic activities was at Teheran, in the Asiatic Games.

Our ties with France are, of course, older—or rather, have never been broken. The King and I, like many of our contemporaries, were given a French education. Furthermore, I think there were special links between my husband and General de Gaulle, a particular friendship which sprang from mutual admiration. When the General came to visit us in 1963, it was an important occasion for Iran. Not only was he the first President of the French Republic to visit us, but he was also a personage of world stature and historic eminence. He enjoyed among us a popularity out of all proportion to what the Iranian people could possibly know of France. He, therefore, received an exceptional welcome.

So much has been written and said about General de Gaulle that it would be difficult to add to his legend. But I shall tell one anecdote which, to my mind, sums him up.

We were at Persepolis and it was very hot—it must have been about midday and the desert sun was very fierce. However, the guide, in his great respect for his visitor, insisted on first telling him, to the last detail, the history of the city of Darius. But the dissertation was never-ending. Everyone was already bathed in sweat and he had only got as far as a meticulous account of the destruction of the town by Alexander when the General, interrupting him with a gesture, said: 'Then, my friend, let us go and see what remains of it!'

Among the letters (by then too late) which reached Colombey-les-Deux-Églises, on the very day after the death of General de Gaulle, was a message from the King . . .

On each of my visits to France, I have always been received with unfailing kindness. In 1974, in Paris, I was accepted as a foreign member of the Académie des Beaux-Arts. I found it very moving as it was, in part, connected with my past studies and because, indirectly, it was a tribute to the effort I was making to promote art in my own country. I was close to tears and there is no doubt that the speech I had to make on that occasion before such an assembly of men of ideas and imagination made me more nervous than any other in my whole life.

It was during this journey, as everyone knows, that the King signed the famous contracts which the Western press was pleased to describe as fabulous. I, of course, was not concerned with that, but rather with the system of insurance and social security. Mme Giscard d'Estaing arranged for me to meet the leading people in that field so that they could explain them to me.

Afterwards, on the way to Les Baux, in Provence, we stopped in a small town and the socialist Deputy for the region lunched with us. In his inimitable southern accent, he told us: 'Our party told us not to come to welcome you, but I am taking no notice. I wanted to see the King and here I am.' It was entirely spontaneous and, to my mind, epitomised the independence of the French character, whatever their political creed.

I was struck by the sincerity of this Deputy throughout

his conversation with the King and I was also very interested in his exchanges with the French Minister accompanying us. He told him: 'You have sent us intellectuals or surgeons as candidates for the Assembly but, you know, there are many more people like me in this town than there are surgeons or intellectuals; you may be sure that most of them will vote for me and not for those others!' Between two serious remarks, there would sometimes flash some goodnatured joke: French humour continues to reserve its rights.

In 1976, the President and Mme Giscard d'Estaing returned our visit. For us, it was an important meeting from every point of view: first of all, for the friendship which existed between the President and the King, then for the special cultural relations which have always linked France and Iran, and finally, because of the considerable economic agreements signed in recent years. We hoped that these meetings would be a success and I think they were.

As usual, all the details had to be checked. The drive from the airport—they had come in a Concorde—was by carriage. But I did not want this to be an opportunity for the launching of personal attacks against M. Giscard d'Estaing and said it must be clearly explained to the press that we received all Heads of State in this manner, whether they came from a communist or socialist country, from a republic or from a monarchy. Then there were those who said a French cook should be engaged, to which I replied: 'Certainly not. It is ridiculous to welcome a French President to Teheran and offer him French cooking. In any case, he certainly would not expect it. We, when we are abroad, eat what is put before us. Our dishes are neither too rich nor too highly-seasoned and I am sure he will enjoy them. And I want no repetition of the criticisms made against us when we brought someone out from Maxim's to Persepolis.' Every time there are masses of details which seem trifling but which, if they are neglected, can accumulate to create an atmosphere quite different from that which was intended.

On that occasion, there was only one incident of which I did not approve. The welcome was pleasant, there were dancers, both men and women, from all the regions, wearing picturesque local costumes, but they chanted invariably: 'Long Live the King! Long Live Giscard!' I felt this was not at all suited to the French taste. I would have liked them to reverse the order from time to time: 'Long Live Giscard! Long Live the King!' or 'Long Live France! Long Live Iran!' or even 'Long Live the President'. It is natural for all Iranians to put the King first, but I thought it might seem a little odd to the French and that they might be left with the impression that it was some kind of personality cult. I also thought that the President of the French Republic might not like to hear 'Long Live Giscard!' too often. I do not know if I was right. To tell the truth, it was really quite unimportant and this visit can be considered a success from every point of view. It certainly strengthened the links between France and Iran. The visit marks the constant progress of our diplomacy. We may sometimes be criticised by people who are ill-informed or of ill will but we maintain the best of relations with most countries of the world.

I do not know how many more miles my life as Queen may cause me to travel, nor how many more Heads of State I shall meet. I cannot say that I know the world as well as I could wish, nor my country as much as I should like. But of one thing I am certain: I still have as much to learn about the modest inhabitants of our own deserts as about the monarchs who preside over the destinies of this world. In all simplicity, I render thanks to my fate for having made it possible for me to meet all these people.

7

...and I am a new wayfarer

I have been Queen now for seventeen years. Seventeen years . . . It is a long time, yet it has passed so quickly. It seems only yesterday I was the young student whom a King was asking in marriage and only the day before that, the little girl pedalling happily along the lanes of Teheran or playing at being a peasant child on the shores of the Caspian . . .

I have been so busy, so few moments have been really my own during these seventeen years, I have so much to do on all the days that God makes that, before this book, I seldom had time to look back, to reflect at such length on the changes I have seen, to concentrate on what I was and on what I have become.

However it may be judged, I have played my part in the forward march of Iran. I have given myself responsibilities and I have tried to bear them. Did I do it for myself or because I am Queen? Doubtless, a little of both, but I think duty usually took precedence over my private life. I have the greatest possible opportunity to be of use and to truly serve my country. If I lived an indolent or frivolous life, I would know no peace. If my destiny had been less exalted, I would have worked, I would have served. It is a need of my nature—but I would have kept a little more time for myself. Yet, of what purpose is life if

128

one does not set a target and, to attain it, go to the very limit of one's abilities?

Now, I am fortunate in not having to worry about material things and can therefore, with an undivided mind, attach real importance to the targets set for my country's progress and to my own efforts to improve myself. 'There, where you are planted, try to flower', I have read somewhere. I have a position, a certain power which allows me to be of use and to do good. And even if the scope of my initiative is sometimes restricted, I remain nonetheless the catalyst of certain intentions, the motivating power which makes certain improvements possible, someone who can make the dreams of others come true.

I cannot keep abreast of everything but when an idea is brought to my notice, if I like it, if I think that to put it into effect will benefit the country, I give it that little push which will free it from bureaucratic red tape. I am proud to have sometimes known how to bring to fruition, with little delay, projects which, without me, would never have reached even the first small step on the road to realisation. Then, where the King is concerned, my wifely duty is to create about him as pleasant an atmosphere as possible, to be careful to avoid family cares being added to those of the State, to help him find relaxation and repose. I also help him in certain fields with which he has not the time to concern himself personally: education, health, culture, social matters . . . Politics are his own personal province but increasingly—it is a sign of the times—they are beginning to affect my own pursuits. Nor must my work make me forget that I am a mother, that I must surround my four children with all my love and take the greatest care of their education, especially that of the Crown Prince. But I also feel like a mother to all our people. I want to remain accessible to all their problems, ready to listen to all those who come to me, whether poor or rich, intellectual or illiterate.

It goes without saying that the attention paid to me is, above all, paid to the King, the powers I have derive from

129

him. And so, before taking an important decision, I always like to speak to him about it first and submit my ideas to him. Sometimes we are of different opinions and then we talk it over; sometimes he succeeds in convincing me or I succeed in convincing him, but there are times when neither of us succeeds in convincing the other. I am very sensitive to certain things and inclined to be carried away and to forget impartiality in pleading a cause close to my heart. I grumble, I criticise . . . The King always tells me that I tackle problems as if they were a matter of life or death. He does not like that very much and it does not help me in whatever it is I want to undertake. I have learned, now, to speak to him calmly, like a responsible and intelligent being. And, of course, if he sees that I am right, he gives the orders necessary for a solution.

Alas, we see far too little of each other for my liking. Lunch is eaten hurriedly, in fifteen or twenty minutes. By the time I sit down to table, my husband has very often finished eating . . . He has to leave, since a busy afternoon lies ahead of him. Then, when he returns from his office, he has stacks of papers to go through. Dinner is usually a family affair and not at all the time to discuss matters of State. Afterwards, the King sometimes plays bridge and then I go back to my office to put my papers in order and prepare for the following day. Sometimes we watch a film together. To avoid tiring him still further after his work, it usually ends with me trying to reserve one of his rare moments of freedom during the next day to talk to him about what I am doing.

In a country where women used to have no position, no power, no opportunity to do their share, it is my duty as the King's wife to set an example of someone who can be, simultaneously, a wife, a mother and someone with duties to discharge. I have to prove that women can also devote themselves usefully to certain activities outside their home and that they must not be divided into categories: those who are educated and 'work', those who are illiterate and keep house. The women of Iran will share with me the benefits that arise from what I do, from any success I obtain. My purpose is to give them courage, to raise them above and out of their obscurity.

I am, by right, the most important woman in the country but I, myself, do not consider that I am of any especial importance. In my opinion, my importance is to be measured by the practical effect of what I say. My words and ideas have their value but if people listen to me, it is because I have the power of the King behind me. My deeds are but a supplementary indication of the esteem accorded me.

I never forget that, as a woman, my position is a delicate one. We are a country where tradition is strong, in which many men have not yet reached the mental and intellectual level to accept unreservedly the admission of women to certain freedoms which they consider perfectly natural for themselves.

In my country, I am considered, whether I like it or not, the representative of feminine emancipation. My strength, the power I wield will, in one way or another, be passed on to all Iranian women. Already these women, formerly regarded as chattels, without the right to be heard, have increasingly more to say for themselves. The fact that the King has granted them the right to vote is beginning to make some headway here and there in certain mentalities. Some regions, however, are slower than others to accept it. It is there, above all, that we must use every means of stirring the imagination.

But although she has suffered many injustices, the Iranian woman has always been a personality. Even if only indirectly, she has exercised influence, a fact which is clear from her elegance and ease of manner. People who have suffered, who have complexes, hold themselves less straight and, to me, the evolution of Iran is measurable by the way in which people carry themselves. Before, they were clumsy, their backs were bent, their heads drooped. Now, they walk upright, their eyes alert, their faces open. It is the barometer of change and development.

The Iranian woman is tender and gentle, she is kind-hearted and hospitable. And I hope that she will preserve all her femininity. Not so long ago, when people talked of a woman who worked, they implied only too readily that, physically, she had become almost masculine. I consider that absurd. A woman who works can very easily retain her grace, she can take decisions and at the same time pay attention to her make-up and her clothes. The one does not exclude the other. It is an outmoded generalisation to think of an elegant, feminine woman as doll-like and an energetic, willing and hard-working woman as a man. When I decided to study architecture, people expected me to return dressed in grey, severely bespectacled, with my hair drawn back into a bun . . . It is true that women who work have less time than others to spend on themselves, but they become increasingly skilful at organising their lives.

Nor must it be forgotten that our peasant women lead harsh lives. In the country, the woman shares all the work on the land and at the same time has to keep house, do the cooking, bring up the children, make bread, fetch water, feed the beasts and then, in her rare moments of freedom, turn to craftsmanship and weave carpets . . . In the North, the woman often works harder than the man, for it is she who plants the rice and gathers the leaves from the tea plant. Despite it all, there is not one without some piece of jewellery, not one who does not take a pride in the embroideries on her blouse.

Nomad women, too, work very hard. After a tiring ride, it is usually they who erect the tents, assemble the kitchens, make the fires and prepare food on the desert stones for the entire clan. They find time to weave, they also know how to shoot and hunt and are fine horsewomen. Until about fifteen years ago, when they were pregnant, they still continued to ride with the caravan, not leaving their horse or camel until the last moment, giving birth to their baby anywhere, picking it up and climbing straight back into the saddle and continuing on their way . . . When they walk, they look like trained models, so straight and elegant are they in their many-coloured dresses. There is nothing about them of the humble, timid woman, who exists only through her husband.

But there is still a long way to go before attitudes of mind are changed. Some Baluchi tribes, for instance, are still very strict with their women: they have neither the right to speak to men, nor to go out. But even there, little by little, progress is being made. Some parents, even if the old uncles do not approve, allow their daughters to attend classes at the rural education centres. Then, they return to the village in uniform and teach their families to drive tractors or to read.

Segregation of the sexes exists in many countries of the Third World. The male child is often better fed than his sister. We must fight to reduce the differences between women and men, between girls and boys, between the young and the old, between the peasant and the town dweller, between one country and another. In Iran, one of the best means of achieving the liberation of women is, without a doubt, national service. Needless to say, our girls do not serve as soldiers, they do not learn to make war. They are more likely to learn office work, but for the sake of discipline and to teach them self-defence, they learn karate or judo. Others, by reason of their studies, serve throughout the country in the Armies of Knowledge, Hygiene and Development.

There are still some laws which must be changed, but our progress must be gradual. We are trying to use tact, to avoid scandalising traditionalists and perhaps provoking a rebound which would set the clock back. For instance, an Iranian woman who wishes to travel and leave the country must still have her husband's permission. But the abolition of this rule is not really a matter of great urgency. It is, rather, a question of pride. The women who really want to leave will always find a means. What is much more serious is the fact that the penal code is very lenient towards the husband who, if he finds his wife in adultery, kills her. Whilst capital punishment exists in Iran for other crimes of bloodshed, such an assassin is given only a light prison sentence. This is intolerable, for it is, in fact, a recognition that there are cases in which people almost have the right to take the law into their own hands. But if this problem is discussed too publicly, the Iranians, strongly traditionist, might think that we are condoning the adultery of women. That would provoke a violent uprising and women would be more confined than ever. If we do not want to compromise for years to come the already very considerable progress made towards feminine emancipation in Iran, we must go forward with great discretion and tact in order to convince people that, in the eyes of the law, there should be no difference between killing one's own wife to avenge masculine pride and assassinating one's neighbour in order to rob him.

Today, when people speak of kings and queens, they immediately think of palaces and carriages, or of bygone days when interest in social matters was non-existent. People find it difficult to imagine that one can be a Queen and still take an interest in the people or work actively for the betterment of one's country. People cling to the legendary vision of queens and princesses without a care in the world, their diadems firmly screwed to their heads, spending all their time changing their dresses, proudly shut away in their splendid mansions. They do not want to know that we, too, are human and, like others, have problems and feelings.

Others sometimes attach much more importance than we do to matters of protocol and the ceremonial of the monarchy. Paradoxically, these same people also expect us to be just like themselves, aware of their difficulties, ready to laugh at their joys and to weep for their sorrows—at once human and super-human. But, if they knew that I, too, work every day, that I, too, have my problems, they might in their heart of hearts reproach me for dimming slightly the fairy-tale image in the *Thousand and One Nights*, which they have invented so that they might dream. Yet that is how it is. I have no particular inclination for the social round and most of my time is spent working, working hard. If a title had to be found for the story of my life which would evoke the legend, it would be far more likely to be *The Thousand and One Days* . . . So much for people's conceptions of the kingdoms of the East. We no longer have pots filled with coins of gold, nor Caliphs, nor Grand Viziers, nor harems filled with sensual sultanas and our carpets no longer fly, except in the baggage lockers of Air Iran . . .

On the other hand, our visitors often arrive prejudiced against us and leave positively enthusiastic. Naturally, that pleases us, but we cannot bring everyone to Iran so that all may have a good impression of the country. When some come to see me and talk to me, they go away saying: 'How nice she was, how very human!' It surprises them, for they did not think it possible. It really is amazing, after so many years, so many visits, speeches, interviews . . . It would be necessary to receive people one at a time to tell them that I, too, have a heart.

Perhaps it is the fault of protocol, but that is a part of tradition and must be respected. There are, of course, those who like to see kings in full panoply and queens wearing a crown. It stirs their imagination, but I am not there to satisfy this imagination, I only conform to custom. When we went to the United States, there was endless talk of 'the Queen in her jewels, the Queen in her jewels!' But these jewels are like a uniform which I must wear; they are not mine, they do not belong to me. Normally, they are deposited in a bank, they are part of the country's wealth, the national patrimony. But I have received letters saying, for instance: 'You have so many jewels on your gowns, you could easily send me a little diamond.' Of course, the stones sewn on to my gowns are not real, but since we come from the East, no one imagines they could be false.

My maid told me once: 'Behind me, in class, there were two girls speaking about you. They said that the Queen bathes twice a day in milk.' Well, they are very young and it amuses them to think that a Queen does extraordinary things but, alas, they are not the only ones. Journalists have often asked me: 'Is it true that you bathe in milk like Cleopatra?' Poor Cleopatra—who knows if she ever bathed in milk! Much of this is doubtless due to the fact that I am never photographed at work. The only photographs published always show me wearing the Crown jewels. Unfortunately, ninety-nine times out of a hundred, people judge by appearances. No one wonders 'What is she, herself, like?' And then they delight in publishing such photographs next to others of some poor peasant. It is very easy to do and possible in any country in the world, even the most advanced. It is for all these reasons that I have gradually begun to wear the royal diadem less and less often. Now, I wear it only for our New Year and the opening of Parliament, or occasionally when we are entertaining sovereigns and I am travelling in countries which are monarchies. I do not wish on such occasions to make myself conspicuous, to appear to be saying: 'What I do is better than what the others do.'

But all that is of little importance. I must admit that I am well aware, through what I hear and what I feel, that the people have a deep affection for me. That is for me the greatest of satisfactions, the greatest of joys. Of course, it is in part due to my activities, but I think that a kind of current has been established between the people and me. Not all Iranians can be completely aware of my work and my anxieties, of what goes on in my head and in my heart; but a sort of hidden contact has been made and I am certain they feel my love and my sincerity. Oddly, the people are more impressed by small gestures of interest or affection than by the great projects we are carrying out: my visits to the lepers, my unexpected arrival at a wrestling match, the kiss I gave an old, infirm village woman. Perhaps there is a particular affection for me because people think that, having myself lived among the people, I understand them better, but there is no doubt that I have also been very fortunate. I became Queen at a time when things were beginning to improve. In short, I entered the life of my country at a propitious moment and—as they say in Iran, where water is so vital—I 'brought the rain with me'. Someone has written 'While the King concerns himself with the GNP (gross national product), the Queen is responsible for the GNH (gross national happiness).' I found this play on words wonderful: it is only by harnessing together progress and happiness, as harmoniously as possible, that we shall become a developed nation. A way of life which has wealth but lacks excellence is as nothing

In twelve years' time, God willing, my son will become King, for my husband has said that he will then abdicate in his favour. Prince Reza will marry and there will be another Queen. My activities will then become less demanding. I hope to retain until then the energy and enthusiasm I have today. I shall age, I shall be more easily tired, but things will proceed under their own momentum. Others, still young today, will, in the natural course of things, take charge.

I shall have more time to myself. I hope I shall not feel too old to enjoy it. I should like to play some instrument reasonably well, to read many books and to draw, to travel without political obligations; in short, everything I do not have the leisure to do at present. Prince Reza will find himself in a very different situation from that which his father inherited thirty-six years ago. Iran is independent and will soon reach the level of the industrialised countries. I do not know exactly how the succession will be arranged, but there is no reason why my son should wait as long as my husband did before being crowned. It may be that it will take place during our lifetimes. That would certainly be, for me, a very great joy.

Prinze Reza's path is marked out, but I should like his sisters and his brother—in addition to some automatic positions they will hold as members of the royal family—to choose a career, to work and to be capable of sailing under their own canvas. What will they be? Doctors, sociologists . . . ? Neither they nor I know yet. The world is changing and I am certain that by the time they reach adult age, they will not find complete satisfaction in being just royalty. It will depend on their characters. Perhaps my daughters will be content with having a husband and raising their children but I would prefer them, in addition to their traditional activities—visits, inaugurations—to choose a particular path for themselves.

As for the régime, I think it has so far been truly useful to Iran. The system will change, perhaps, a little, the relationship between the citizens and the ruling power will develop, the responsibilities will be better distributed. The manner in which the King guides the country, the creation of the new party, have as their purpose to give the people an increasing share in the political life of Iran. It is our wish that a true democracy should be established before long, not a copy of the other democracies in the world, but one which will correspond as closely as possible to the aspirations of the people of Iran. Today, the country has need of a King, of his power, his intelligence, his leadership. As history has already proved, the monarchy will exist so long as the country and the people consider it to be of use to them. I cannot say if it will come to an end or if it will continue for as long again as it has already existed but, if one thinks about it, it is a fact that the most advanced countries in the world are monarchies: the Netherlands, Belgium, Sweden, Norway, Denmark . . . Why? Because they have dynastic continuity. In Iran, the Head of State is above the manoeuvres of politicians, he thinks only of the inmost being of the country and of its future.

In our present system, everything is too dependent on the King. This must be changed. The people do not assume enough of the responsibilities. They are like children who have always been pampered by their parents. When the parents die, the children are lost. It is the King's wish that, when he goes, the country should be capable of continuing to progress. More time is still needed to reach that point, the time when Ministers, worried by some detail, do not come to refer it to the King.

Sometimes, through the fault of those who are unwilling to shoulder responsibility, our orders are badly carried out or misinterpreted. An example? I hate neon lights and advertisements in flashing lights. For some, they represent progress, but for me, they signify decadence, and tree-lined streets are too often disfigured by them. Now, on one of my provincial tours, I saw one of these signs hiding some very fine trees. I asked the Governor: 'Tell the shopkeeper to take it down and set it further back. If any expense is involved, the municipality will pay it.' The next day, the Governor demolished this poor man's sign: that is how my words were interpreted. I had wanted to do something good to embellish the town, but if the shopkeeper had asked the Governor why he was doing it, the latter would have replied: 'It is the Queen who has ordered your sign to be pulled down.' There is no doubt I emerged from it all diminished in the eyes of the people, quite the opposite of what I had intended.

The details with which I concern myself are inconceivable. For example, it was I who had to approve the plan for a new hotel in Shiraz and give my opinion on whether or not bidets should be fitted. Then there were refuse bins to be chosen for the streets of Teheran. What a waste of time and energy! I sometimes tell myself that it is our own fault, that we should say far more often: 'I am not prepared to take on this problem, I have no opinion to give you, get on with it yourselves.'

Without a true division of responsibilities, there will be no democracy, at least, not in the sense in which we understand the word. Great Britain, the United States and France consider themselves to be democratic countries, the Soviet Union and the Eastern countries call themselves democratic republics, yet they have nothing at all in common. Democracy means that each individual can give his opinion and take charge of his own destiny, as well as that of his country. Basically, as the King says, what matters is the one per cent above fifty which creates a majority. But when one watches the manner in which elections are held in certain countries, the lengths to which politicians will go in order to win a few more votes, it is not exactly attractive. It is a matter of inventing a gadget here to attract the housewives, a formula there to attract the intellectuals, rather than of planning major projects for the country. I call it fraudulent.

Iran will need a King for a long time yet, a force which symbolises the nation, a continuity in its culture. It is desirable, if one examines the fate of certain other peoples: one day there is a president, the next day he is assassinated; one group seizes power: a week later, there is a *coup d'état*. Those who govern never have long enough to really get to know the problems and to achieve progress. The country does not have an opportunity to develop. Because of its geographical situation, I think that Iran without a King would be unbelievably chaotic.

Clearly, everything depends on the will of a country, for it is difficult to maintain a régime which the people reject. But I find it difficult to imagine a republic in Iran. When the King's father achieved his *coup d'état*, he wanted to establish a republic, but public opinion prevented him. It refused to accept the abolition of the monarchy and wanted him to become King. It was, in any case, eminently sensible. In fifty years, Iran has had only two Heads of State and it is that which has made possible its stability and its progress. Would the country have emerged so fast from the Middle Ages to plunge into the atomic age if, during the same period, it had had twelve presidents, with all the changes of policy which that would have entailed?

Furthermore, there is a unique spiritual relationship between a people and its King, as between a father and his children. Of course, it is desirable for everyone that Iran should have a good King, but, even if he were not so, a bad King would not be able to commit the errors or extortions that were possible four hundred years ago—we now have a government and elected representatives of the people—and he would at least have the merit of upholding, merely by his presence, the unity of the country. In any case, this is how our people understands its monarchy and the reason why it remains so deeply attached to it.

This national 'cement' is not a figment of the imagination. After an earthquake, I appealed to the nation for help for the victims and the people's response was truly tremendous. For me, it was a great joy to see that the Iranians were so united and that if a misfortune hit the country, they were all there to lend a hand. The leaders of industry gave huge sums, but I saw other gestures, extraordinary in a quite different way: children who broke open their money-boxes, a workman who came empty-handed but took off his jacket to give it to the victims, a woman who brought a cracked frying-pan—it probably represented half her kitchen equipment. This generosity and solidarity in a moment of stress bodes well for the future.

Clearly, not all mentalities are yet properly attuned to modern times. I have been told—I do not know if it is true, but it is, in any case, significant—that an Iranian actor one day found all the windows of his house broken. In a film, he had played the part of a man who killed his mother and some of the audience—somewhat confused between reality and cinematographic fiction—had come to show, in this way, their horror at the terrible crime . . . It is but natural, for our progress has now advanced beyond the average comprehension. At the beginning of the century, everyone knew how a horse and cart functioned but today, how many passengers in jet aeroplanes understand the mechanism which propels them through the air? In any case, it is not only here that such things happen: when *The Longest Day* was being filmed in Normandy, the French actors refused to wear German uniforms. All that is very human and of no particular importance. Increased access to learning and the spread of education—if it is able to keep pace with events—can, in one generation, overcome all the barriers. And, in any case, our country is going resolutely forward.

What distresses me far more at this moment is the bad reputation of Iran abroad. This adverse publicity, based on political prisoners and tortures, is terribly unjust. It is truly dreadful to attack a country and a system so relentlessly. The accusations made against us are grotesque. The smallest incident is like a snowball which, from country to country and from one newspaper to the next, grows out of all proportion and becomes an avalanche.

It is just one more trial. Nothing in life is easy, not even for a Queen, contrary to what many people may think. I am very busy, I work very hard, often with great energy, joy and enthusiasm, but there are also moments when I am very tired, when so much injustice depresses me. Then I feel that everything is going wrong, that it is the end of the world and I am desolate. But I soon recover, I recall the immense progress we are achieving and tell myself that very soon no one will be able, without appearing ridiculous, to pretend not to see it. The attitude of Western intellectuals towards us will then be forced to change.

But sometimes it is hard. I have many women friends, my mother, my husband, an aunt to whom I confide many things, but in the end, in our position, faced with great problems, one is often alone. It is more or less the lot of all human beings, but I must never forget that I am Queen and that, although I know so many secrets, there is no one with whom I may share all my cares, no one to whom I can tell everything. A little to one, a little to another, I have not the right to give those about me more of myself than that.

I often speak of a certain philosophy with which I hope to imbue my life, of spirituality, but I tell myself from time to time that it is perhaps easier for me than for others because all my material needs are met, I can have anything I want. Then I try to forget who I am and to put myself in the place of a modest couple who earn a small living, to see if I would preach the same attitude. Are people right to kill themselves with overwork in order to have a little more money, to buy a house, another house, a car, another car? I think that if my situation were more humble, my reply would be the same. I can allow myself to stand above things and have a moral obligation to do so. Whether through simple humanity or religious feeling, it is also my duty to be just, to forgive, to forget and to serve. If the first reaction to offence is to return blow for blow, it is too easy in my position to take revenge and do a great deal of harm. That is why, for me—since I have the power—it is far more important not to do so.

To tell the truth, I find the best examples of humanity

among ordinary people. There are those who, by the strength of their personality, because they are as they are, give one courage and hope in mankind. I have one quite recent memory: I went incognito to the southern part of Teheran, to an area where there is a certain problem. The area is outside the city limits, in a zone where no one is allowed to build, yet people are settling there and building houses. The municipality pulls them down, but they are rebuilt at night with bricks and enveloped in plastic sheets. People dwell there in extremely bad conditions and, as I had received many reports on the matter, I decided to see for myself what the situation was. With those accompanying me, I met a woman washing her linen in the courtyard. Immediately, without recognising me, she said to us: 'Come, I will give you tea. Come and see my house.' This straightforwardness, this kindness, this hospitality of the humble, this is what I like above all else. I have a far greater admiration for people like this than for all the politicians of the world and rank them in my heart with artists and thinkers, those who have a care for the beauty, the culture, the present state of the world and its future.

What am I beside them? Sometimes, we go to a concert hall or a stadium and each time we are greeted with cheers. My first reaction is to return the greeting, to reply to the waving. Then I think that, if I allow myself to show my feelings too openly, it is arrogating importance to myself, taking to myself all the applause which is really given to my office. So I do not make many gestures in reply and take my seat at once. But afterwards I think the spectators may believe I am taking no notice of them, that I am haughty, whereas, in fact, it is really embarrassment at being always applauded. It is a form of modesty. But I do have to respond because people expect it of me. If I did not, no one would understand that it might have been from shyness.

When I am travelling in our provinces, I often have the same feeling. I know there are many who want to see me and I tell myself that if I remain seated in the depths of the car, those at the back of the crowd will not even catch a glimpse of me and will have come for nothing. So I stand up and remain standing in the car. There again, I feel I am giving myself importance and it irks me. At the same time, I know that it gives the people pleasure, that they have perhaps been waiting hours for that moment.

At heart, one always remains oneself. The title does not change one's inner self. For others, I am the Empress and that is heavy with meaning, but for myself, I am the same person as before and despite all the respect about me, all the honours I am accorded, I do not feel important.

Sometimes we go to Europe to ski and everything is quite different. People do not recognise us and we live rather like everyone else. I like living like that and for me it is a real escape to be able to walk through the streets, to do the simplest things, to go into a shop or a restaurant. After a while, if someone looks at me, I wonder why. When I live like that, I even forget who I am.

It is sometimes tiring to be endlessly watched. The slightest gesture, the least word, everything you do, all that you say is watched, analysed, registered, filmed. It is rather as if our entire life were led in front of the cameras. I miss the anonymity of earlier years.

I have had my share of life, of its good things and its bad. With the passing of time, we fortunately recall only the best memories. My life has always been so full and I have done so many things that, at the age of thirty-eight, I feel sixty. Imam Ali said: 'You should work as if you were going to die tomorrow and also as if you were going to live eternally'. I have tried to give all that it is in my power to give. My intelligence, my love, my energy, all that I have within me, I have tried to express. If I have succeeded, if I have brought something to my country, so much the better, for I have done all that I could and could not have done more. Perhaps I should have appeared more brilliant, invented wonderful projects, worked differently, but I have only the abilities given me by nature. I have tried to cultivate the qualities within me which are productive and to subdue those which are not.

So far as my personal education is concerned, my only ambition is this: to use to the limit the qualities which I, like every living being, possess and to conquer the faults which, like everyone else, I must endure.

I look forward to the day when I shall feel truly at peace with myself. To achieve that requires much trouble and effort. It comes gradually, one must advance step by step, sometimes climbing one step and falling two, but picking oneself up and carrying on.

I sometimes wonder why we live, why we take such great pains. To what purpose? There are in my life so many objectives to attain, so many things to bring to completion but the search is in other fields, too: to discover a certain transcendence so that life may assume its full meaning.

Otherwise, I have had the highest position, fame and popularity, I have had all the money I wanted, all the gowns and jewels I desired, I have made great journeys. But when one is involved in so many things, when one's own development is linked to that of one's country, it is not these things which are important. One's duty is to live like a real human being and not to allow life to dominate, crush and humiliate you.

My happiness does not lie in having everything I want. I cannot say to myself: 'Now I have that, I want nothing more.' After my personal preoccupations come my ambitions for the country; after my preoccupation with the country there is my anxiety for the world, with nuclear weapons, famine, poverty, wars. Will there one day be a planet Earth that is happy, where everyone can live in peace? Such is my life: I pass without transition from some small detail of my own daily life to a problem which concerns the whole world. It is endless. When I stop worrying for a moment about my country or international relations, I wonder about the future of my children. What will their lives be, and then, too, what will be my own future, what will be the future of the King, of the monarchy? Afterwards, I tell myself: 'Instead of worrying about the future, do all you can and let the future take care of itself.'

145

I like to re-read these lines of Hafez which I have
written on the fly-leaf of my notebook:

> *All-powerful, let the spirit of justice*
> *Be my faithful companion on the journey,*
> *For the way is long*
> *And I am a new wayfarer.*